SPAIN & PORTUGAL

TRAVEL GUIDE

2025

The Comprehensive tips to explore the Iberian Peninsula Best cites with everything you need to know

2in1

SONIA DAVIS

COPYRIGHT
BY
SONIA DAVIS
All rights reserved. No part of this publication may be reproduced, distributed, or transmitted in any form or by any means, including photocopying, recording, or other electronic or mechanical methods, without the prior written permission of the publisher, except in the case of brief quotations embodied in critical reviews and certain other non-commercial uses permitted by copyright law

DISCLAIMER

This guide is based on my personal experiences and extensive research conducted with local experts. While every effort has been made to ensure the accuracy and reliability of the information provided, prices, availability, and other details are subject to change without notice. Readers are encouraged to verify any critical information before making travel plans, as circumstances may vary.
The author and publisher are not responsible for any losses, damages, or inconveniences arising from the use of this guide. Traveling involves risks, and it is essential to stay informed about local laws, customs, and safety guidelines.

3 *SPAIN & PORTUGAL TRAVEL GUIDE*

TABLE OF CONTENTS

TRAVEL PLANS 10

Common Mistakes to avoid 10
Lodging Consideration: 12
Packing and equipment guide: 14
Dealing with get lag and fatigue 18
Local expert 19

INTRODUCTION TO SPAIN 21

CHAPTER 1: WHAT NOT TO DO IN SPAIN 23

CHAPTER 2: TRANSPORTATION 25

Going to Spain. 25
Getting Around Spain: 26

CHAPTER 3: LANGUAGE AND COMMUNICATION 30

Basic Spanish phrases to communicate with the local 30

CHAPTER 4: MADRID 36

CHINCHÓN 36

   Top 3 Luxury Hotels in Chinchón 36
   Top 4 Mid-Range and Low Budget Stays in Chinchón 37
   Where to Eat in Chinchón 39
   Coffee and Café Shops in Chinchón 40
   Bars, Nightlife, and Entertainment in Chinchón 40

SAN LORENZO DE EL ESCORIAL 42

Museums and Galleries in Madrid 47

Historical Sites in Madrid 52

Hiking in Madrid 56

CHAPTER 5: BARCELONA 59

SITGES 59

Top 3 Luxury Hotels in Sitges 59

Top 4 Mid-Range and Low-Budget Stays 60

Where to Eat in Sitges 61

Coffee and Café Shops in Sitges 62

Bars, Nightlife, and Entertainment 63

CADAQUÉS 63

Museums and Galleries in Barcelona 68

Historical Sites in Barcelona: 72

Parks and Gardens in Barcelona 75

CHAPTER 6: VALENCIA 78

CHULILLA 78

ALTEA 82

Museums and Galleries in Valencia 86

Historical Sites in Valencia 89

Parks and Gardens in Valencia 92

CHAPTER 7: SEVILLE 95

ALCALÁ DE GUADAÍRA 95

CARMONA 100

Museums and Galleries in Seville 104

Historical Sites in Seville 106

CHAPTER 8: GRANADA 110

PAMPANEIRA 110

SALOBREÑA 114

Tourism Centers in Granada 119

Museums and Galleries in Granada 120

Parks and Gardens in Granada 121

CHAPTER 9: WHAT TO DO IN SPAIN 123

Spain's Festivals 123

Top 10 Local Cuisine to Try in Spain 126

CHAPTER 10: 7 DAYS ITINERARY IN SPAIN 132

FROM SPAIN TO PORTUGAL 137

Required Documents for Traveling from Spain to Portugal .. 137

Plane to Portugal 138

Train to Portugal 139

Private Car or Personal Guide 140

Best Routes and Travel Times 141

    Madrid to Lisbon: 141

    Barcelona to Porto: 141

    Seville to Faro: 142

INTRODUCTION TO PORTUGAL 144

CHAPTER 1: WHAT NOT TO DO IN PORTUGAL 148

CHAPTER 2: PORTO 152

RIBEIRA 152
VILA NOVA DE GAIA 158
BOAVISTA 163
Museums and Galleries in Porto 169
Historical Sites in Porto 171
CHAPTER 3: LISBON 174
ALFAMA 174
BAIRRO ALTO 180
Museums and Galleries in Lisbon 187
Historical Sites in Lisbon: 189
CHAPTER 4: COIMBRA 192
Museums and Galleries in Coimbra 198
Historical Sites in Coimbra 200
CHAPTER 5: WHAT TO DO IN PORTUGAL 203
FESTIVALS TO PARTICIPATE IN 203
PORTUGAL LOCAL CUISINE TO TRY 208
BEACHES TO EXPLORE 212
HIKING AND WALKING TRAIL IN PORTUGAL 217
Portuguese language to interact with the local 225
CHAPTER 6: 7 DAYS ITINERARY IN PORTUGAL 230
CHAPTER 7: HEALTH AND SAFETY RULES 233
Spain and Portugal for Aged 60 and Above 235

CHAPTER 8: BONUS 239

Cost breakdown for different travel style 239

CONCLUSION 244

9 *SPAIN & PORTUGAL TRAVEL GUIDE*

TRAVEL PLANS

Common Mistakes to avoid

Failure to Confirm Visa Requirements: Different countries have varying visa regulations. Not confirming these requirements in advance can lead to being denied entry. It's also essential to check passport validity, as some countries have strict rules on how long a passport must be valid beyond the travel date.

Lack of Sufficient Funds: Traveling without enough savings can cause financial strain, making it difficult to cover unexpected expenses. Ensuring a well-planned budget, including emergencies, is critical to avoid running out of money during the trip.

Overpacking: Packing unnecessary items like clothes or shoes can waste effort, energy, and money. Overpacking creates unnecessary strain when moving around, especially when navigating non-ADA compliant locations with heavy luggage. Travelers should research the climate of their destination and pack only what is necessary.

Failure to Have Hard Copies of Reservations: Relying solely on digital copies without a backup can cause challenges, especially if data connections fail. Printing or downloading reservations ensures you have access to vital information.

Overscheduling: Travelers often overschedule their itineraries, not factoring in delays caused by airport logistics, transportation, and getting settled at their destination.

Unrealistic Expectations of Sleep on Flights: Expecting to sleep well on long flights, even in first-class, is unrealistic, leading to exhaustion upon arrival.

Failure to Purchase Travel Insurance: Travel insurance is important to cover emergency expenses, such as medical issues, ensuring you are prepared for unforeseen circumstances.

Ignoring Travel Time and Dates: Misreading the itinerary and arrival times, especially when crossing time zones (+1 or +2 days), can lead to confusion with bookings and schedules.

Trying to Do Too Much: Travelers often try to visit too many destinations, leading to a blurred and overwhelming experience, especially on their first trip.

Traveling During Crowded Seasons: Traveling during peak tourist seasons can result in overcrowded attractions, higher prices, and limited availability for accommodations. To avoid these challenges, plan trips during off-peak seasons when possible, for a more relaxed and affordable experience.

Lodging Consideration:

When planning a trip, choosing the right accommodation is a key decision that can shape your entire experience. Travelers have various options, ranging from luxury accommodations to low-budget stays. Making the right choice depends on your budget, preferences, and travel goals.

Luxury Accommodations

Luxury hotels and accommodations offer a level of comfort, convenience, and service that is unrivaled. If you have a substantial budget, opting for luxury hotels can transform your trip into a truly lavish experience. These accommodations often come with premium amenities like spacious rooms, top-notch restaurants, spa services, fitness centers, and 24-hour room service. You can expect personalized service, such as concierge assistance, which makes navigating a new city easier. Additionally, luxury hotels are typically located in prime areas, giving you easy access to the best attractions, restaurants, and shopping districts.

One of the significant advantages of luxury accommodations is the privacy, peace, and relaxation they offer. For business travelers or those seeking a quiet retreat, this can make a difference in productivity or rejuvenation. However, luxury comes at a price. It's crucial to ensure that your budget can sustain such expenses without causing financial strain, as luxury hotels can be quite expensive.

Low-Budget Stays

For travelers who prefer to save money, low-budget stays such as hostels, guesthouses, or budget hotels are ideal. These accommodations often provide basic amenities, including clean rooms, Wi-Fi, and sometimes a complimentary breakfast. Low-budget options are especially attractive to backpackers, students, or anyone traveling on a tight budget. They allow you to save money that can be better spent on experiences, such as sightseeing, dining, or local tours.

One of the major advantages of low-budget stays is the opportunity to meet fellow travelers. Many hostels have common areas where guests can socialize, share travel tips, or even make lifelong friends. Staying in low-budget accommodations can also immerse you in local cultures and neighborhoods that might not be accessible in more luxurious areas.

Making Accommodation Decisions

When choosing between luxury and low-budget stays, consider your budget, the purpose of your trip, and your personal preferences. If you have enough money and want to indulge, luxury hotels can enhance your experience. On the other hand, if you need to stick to a budget, low-budget accommodations will allow you to travel without breaking the bank.

Packing and equipment guide:

When traveling to destinations like Spain and Portugal, it's important to pack smartly to ensure a comfortable and enjoyable trip. Here's a list of travel essentials to consider bringing along:

1. Travel Documents:

- Passport: Ensure it has at least six months of validity remaining.
- Visa (if applicable): Check if you need a visa for either country.
- Travel insurance: For medical coverage, lost luggage, or trip cancellation.
- Hotel reservations: Printed or digital copies.
- Flight tickets: Printed or stored on your phone.
- Copies of important documents: In case of loss (passport, insurance, etc.).

2. Money and Cards:

- Credit and debit cards: Ensure they work internationally and inform your bank of your travel plans.
- Local currency (Euros): To cover small expenses upon arrival.
- Travel wallet: To organize cash, cards, and documents securely.

3. Clothing:

- Lightweight, breathable clothing: Spain and Portugal can be hot, especially in summer.

- Comfortable walking shoes: Cobblestone streets are common.
- Layers: Evenings can be cooler, so pack a light jacket or sweater.
- Swimwear: For beaches, pools, or hot springs.
- Sun protection: Sunglasses, a hat, and sunscreen are essential.
- Rain gear: A compact umbrella or light raincoat for unexpected rain showers.

4. Toiletries and Personal Care Items:

- Travel-sized toiletries: Shampoo, conditioner, body wash, toothbrush, toothpaste, etc.
- Moisturizer: For dry skin after sun exposure.
- Deodorant: Preferably travel-sized.
- Medications: Any prescription or over-the-counter medicine you regularly take.
- First aid kit: With band-aids, antiseptic, and any basic medicine like ibuprofen.

5. Technology and Gadgets:

- Mobile phone and charger: Ensure you have international roaming or a local SIM card.
- Portable power bank: To keep your devices charged on the go.
- Travel adapter: Spain and Portugal use Type C and F plugs, with 230V.
- Camera: To capture your travels, though many use their phone for this.
- E-reader or book: For entertainment during downtime or travel.

6. Navigation and Entertainment:
- Maps or a GPS app: Google Maps or offline maps for navigating the cities.
- Travel guides or language apps: To help with local phrases in Spanish or Portuguese.

7. Miscellaneous:
- Reusable water bottle: Stay hydrated, especially in hot weather.
- Daypack: For daily excursions and exploring.
- Snacks: Especially for long train rides or while exploring.

- Beach towel: For coastal destinations in Spain and Portugal.
- Lock for luggage: For added security at hostels or budget stays.

8. Cultural and Local Essentials:
- Modest clothing: For visiting religious sites (cathedrals, churches, etc.).
- Phrasebook or translation app: While English is widely spoken, learning a few words in Spanish or Portuguese can be useful and appreciated.

By packing these essentials, you'll be well-prepared for a memorable trip to Spain and Portugal!

Dealing with get lag and fatigue

Dealing with jet lag and fatigue is essential for ensuring an enjoyable travel experience, especially when crossing multiple time zones. Jet lag occurs when your internal body clock struggles to adjust to a new time zone, leading to fatigue, sleep disturbances, and difficulty concentrating.

To manage jet lag, begin adjusting your sleep schedule a few days before departure. Gradually shift your sleeping and eating times to align with your destination's time zone. Once on the flight, try to rest and stay hydrated by drinking water instead of caffeine or alcohol, which can worsen dehydration and fatigue.

Upon arrival, spend time outdoors in natural sunlight. Sunlight helps regulate your body's circadian rhythm, making it easier to adjust. If possible, avoid naps, especially in the afternoon, and stay awake until the local bedtime to sync your sleep cycle.

Additionally, stay active by walking or stretching during the day to combat fatigue and enhance circulation. Eating light, balanced meals can also support energy levels and prevent sluggishness. Finally, give your body time to adapt; for every time zone crossed, it can take about a day to fully adjust. Being patient and taking care of your health will help you recover quickly from jet lag and enjoy your trip.

Local expert

When visiting Spain or Portugal for the first time, it can be beneficial to hire a tour guide or travel companion to help you navigate the destination. These individuals are well-versed in the local culture, history, and landmarks, ensuring you get the most out of your trip. You can find trustworthy guides through reputable travel agencies, certified tourism websites, or by seeking recommendations from reliable sources.

It's important to exercise caution when choosing a guide. Always confirm their credentials, such as certifications or affiliations with recognized tourism boards, to avoid being scammed. Additionally, checking online reviews from previous clients can help ensure you're dealing with a reputable guide. Be wary of individuals offering their services spontaneously without proper verification. Booking through well-established platforms or directly through your accommodation is a safer route to finding a dependable and knowledgeable guide. I suggest hiring a guide if you're seeking a more in-depth experience or if you're traveling solo and require extra insights beyond what this book provides.

INTRODUCTION TO SPAIN

Spain, officially known as the Kingdom of Spain, is a vibrant and diverse country located in southwestern Europe. Occupying roughly 85 percent of the Iberian Peninsula, which it shares with its smaller neighbor Portugal, Spain is a land of rich history, stunning landscapes, and distinct regional cultures. Its heartland is dominated by the Meseta, a high plateau flanked by majestic mountain ranges such as the Pyrenees to the north and the Sierra Nevada to the south. Spain's geographical diversity is mirrored by its cultural richness, where ancient traditions blend seamlessly with modern life.

Historically, Spain has been shaped by a multitude of civilizations. Roman conquerors left behind roads, language, and monuments, and many of Rome's greatest emperors, including Trajan and Hadrian, were Spanish. The Moors ruled large parts of the country for nearly 800 years, contributing to Spain's architectural splendor and advancing its sciences and poetry. Following the fall of Moorish rule, Spain embarked on its Golden Age in the 15th and 16th centuries, fueled by exploration and the discovery of the Americas under Christopher Columbus in 1492.

Spain's vast empire made it one of the most powerful nations in the world, although its influence waned over the centuries.

Culturally, Spain is a mosaic of traditions, from the flamenco rhythms of Andalusia to the vibrant festivals of Valencia and the unique identity of Catalonia. The country has produced world-renowned artists like Pablo Picasso and Salvador Dalí, and its cities, such as Madrid and Barcelona, are hubs of artistic and intellectual life. Spain's cuisine, too, is famed for its regional diversity, from the seafood paella of Valencia to the hearty stews of Castile. Whether through its historical landmarks like the Alhambra in Granada or its bustling modern metropolises, Spain offers a captivating blend of the old and the new, making it one of Europe's most alluring destinations.

CHAPTER 1: WHAT NOT TO DO IN SPAIN

Dining Delays: Expect late meal times; lunch is usually 1 PM–3:30 PM, and dinner starts after 9 PM, especially in summer.

Relaxed Attitudes: Spanish culture values a laid-back approach to time; don't stress about punctuality.

Regional Sensitivity: Avoid discussing regionalism as it can be sensitive, particularly in regions like Catalonia and the Basque Country.

Beyond the Costa del Sol: Explore other beautiful coasts in Spain, such as Costa de la Luz, instead of just the touristy Costa del Sol.

Identity and Culture: Respect local identities, like not calling Catalans "Spanish," and seek authentic Flamenco performances primarily in Andalusia.

Packing Smart: Spain has excellent shopping options; consider leaving space in your luggage for new purchases.

Socializing at the Bar: Sit at the bar in tapas bars for a lively experience and to engage with locals and staff.

Exploring Lesser-Known Regions: Venture beyond major cities to discover the rich culture in smaller towns and rural areas.

Dressing Appropriately: Dress respectfully, avoiding beachwear in public areas to adhere to local customs.

Embracing Local Markets: Visit local markets for fresh produce and local delicacies, immersing yourself in the culture.

Flexible Itinerary: Allow spontaneity in your travel plans to discover unexpected treasures and experiences.

Enjoying Hot Chocolate, the Local Way: Dip churros in thick Spanish hot chocolate instead of drinking it straight.

Avoiding Tourist Resorts: Step beyond tourist resorts for a more authentic and culturally rich experience in Spain.

Discovering the Mountains: Explore Spain's mountains, which offer unique outdoor activities like hiking and skiing.

Cultural Etiquette: Be aware of local superstitions, such as bad luck associated with passing salt and the unluckiness of Tuesdays.

CHAPTER 2: TRANSPORTATION

Going to Spain.

If you're planning to visit Spain, understanding visa requirements and booking an international flight are crucial steps. Spain is part of the Schengen Zone, so travelers from many countries need a Schengen visa to enter. If you're from a country that requires a visa, ensure you apply well in advance. The application process typically involves filling out a form, submitting a valid passport, providing travel insurance, proof of accommodation, and a return flight ticket. You may also need to show proof of financial means to support your stay. It's advised to apply for a visa at least a month before your trip, as processing times vary depending on your country of residence and the consulate's workload.

When it comes to flights, Spain's main international airport is Adolfo Suárez Madrid-Barajas Airport (MAD) in Madrid. Other major international airports include Barcelona El Prat Airport (BCN) and Málaga-Costa del Sol Airport (AGP). It's recommended to book your international flight several months in advance to secure the best fares, especially if you're traveling during peak tourist seasons like summer. Many international airlines operate direct flights to Spain, so compare fares and check luggage allowances, as well as arrival times, to ensure a smooth journey.

Getting Around Spain:

When planning a visit to Spain, it's essential to understand how to access various towns from the main international airports in Madrid, Barcelona, Valencia, Seville, and Granada. Each airport provides convenient transportation options, allowing travelers to explore the surrounding regions with ease.

Accessing Towns from Madrid Airport (Adolfo Suárez Madrid-Barajas Airport)
Chinchón is located approximately 50 km from Madrid and can be reached by bus on line 337 from Conde de Casal or by car, taking around 45 minutes. Alcalá de Henares, a historic university town, is about 30 km away, accessible via the Cercanías C2 or C7 train from Atocha station, with a travel time of around 45 minutes, or a 30-minute drive by car. For those heading to San Lorenzo de El Escorial, which is about 60 km from the capital, trains on the Cercanías C3 line from Atocha or Chamartín stations take about

an hour, while driving takes approximately 50 minutes. Lastly, Manzanares el Real, another picturesque town located 50 km away, can be accessed by bus on line 724 from Plaza de Castilla or by car in about 45 minutes.

Transportation from Barcelona Airport (Barcelona-El Prat Airport)
From Barcelona, travelers can easily reach Sitges, located 40 km away, via train on the Rodalies R2 line from Sants station or by car in roughly 35 minutes. The stunning coastal town of Cadaqués is further away, approximately 170 km, and can be reached by bus from Barcelona Nord Station or a 2.5-hour drive. To get to Begur, located 130 km from Barcelona, travelers can take a bus from Estació del Nord to Palafrugell, then a short ride to Begur, or drive in about 1 hour and 45 minutes. Figueres, known for the Salvador Dalí Theatre-Museum, is about 140 km from Barcelona and is accessible by the high-speed Renfe AVE train to Figueres-Vilafant station or a 1.5-hour drive.

Getting to Towns from Valencia Airport (Valencia Airport)

From Valencia, Chulilla is around 60 km away and can be reached by car in about an hour or by bus from Estació del Nord. Altea, situated 140 km from Valencia, requires a train to Alicante followed by a tram to Altea, or a drive of approximately 1 hour and 45 minutes. Buñol, famous for its annual tomato festival, is just 40 km away, accessible by train on the Cercanías C3 line or a 40-minute drive. Peñíscola, another beautiful coastal town, is located 140 km from Valencia, with travel options including a train to Benicarló-Peñíscola station followed by a taxi or bus, or a drive taking about 1 hour and 30 minutes.

Transportation from Seville Airport (Seville Airport)

Alcalá de Guadaíra is only 15 km from Seville, reachable by bus (M-121 from Prado de San Sebastián) or a quick 20-minute drive by car. Carmona, located 30 km away, can be accessed via bus from Prado de San Sebastián or by car in 30 minutes. For a visit to Cazalla de la Sierra, which is 90 km from Seville, bus services from Plaza de Armas take about 1 hour and 20 minutes, while driving is an option too. Alfalfa, a neighborhood within Seville, is just 10 km away, easily accessible by taxi or local bus from the city center.

Accessing Towns from Granada Airport (Federico García Lorca Granada-Jaén Airport)

In Granada, travelers can reach Pampaneira, located 75 km away, via bus from Granada or by car in about 1 hour and 15 minutes. Salobreña is approximately 65 km from Granada, accessible by bus from the Granada bus station or a 50-minute drive. Alhama de Granada, located 55 km away, can be reached by bus or a 1-hour drive from Granada. Lastly, Guadix, 60 km from Granada, offers access via train from the Granada train station or a 50-minute drive.

For most of these towns, renting a car provides flexibility for exploring at your own pace. However, buses and trains serve as efficient and affordable alternatives for travelers who prefer public transportation. This comprehensive guide ensures a seamless travel experience while discovering the charming towns of Spain.

CHAPTER 3: LANGUAGE AND COMMUNICATION

Basic Spanish phrases to communicate with the local

Here are some common Spanish phrases to help you communicate with locals in various situations, along with how they're spoken.

Greetings & Basic Conversations:

- Hello – "Hola"
- (oh-lah)

- Good morning – "Buenos días"
- (bweh-nohs dee-ahs)

- Good afternoon – "Buenas tardes"
- (bweh-nahs tar-des)

- Good evening/night – "Buenas noches"
- (bweh-nahs noh-ches)

- How are you? – "¿Cómo estás?"
- (koh-moh es-tahs)

- I'm fine, thank you – "Estoy bien, gracias"
- (es-toy byen, grah-thyahs)

- What's your name? – "¿Cómo te llamas?"
- (koh-moh teh yah-mahs)

- My name is... – "Me llamo..."
- (meh yah-moh)

- Nice to meet you – "Mucho gusto"
- (moo-choh goos-toh)

Asking for Help/Information:

- Excuse me – "Perdón"
- (pehr-dohn)

- Can you help me? – "¿Me puedes ayudar?"
- (meh pweh-des ah-yoo-dar)

- Where is…? – "¿Dónde está…?"
- (dohn-deh es-tah)

- How much does it cost? – "¿Cuánto cuesta?"
- (kwan-toh kwes-tah)

- I don't understand – "No entiendo"
- (noh en-tyen-doh)

- Do you speak English? – "¿Hablas inglés?"
- (ah-blahs een-gles)

Ordering at a Restaurant:

- I would like... – "Quisiera..."
- (kee-syeh-rah)

- A table for two, please – "Una mesa para dos, por favor"
- (oo-nah meh-sah pah-rah dos, por fah-vohr)

- The menu, please – "El menú, por favor"
- (ehl meh-noo, por fah-vohr)

- Water – "Agua"
- (ah-gwah)

- Check, please – "La cuenta, por favor"
- (lah kwen-tah, por fah-vohr)

Directions & Transportation:

- Where is the bus/train station? – "¿Dónde está la estación de autobuses/tren?"
- (dohn-deh es-tah lah es-tah-syon deh ow-toh-boo-ses/trehn)

- Left/Right – "Izquierda/Derecha"
- (ees-kyehr-dah/deh-reh-chah)

- Straight ahead – "Todo recto"
- (toh-doh reh-toh)

- I need a taxi – "Necesito un taxi"
- (neh-seh-see-toh oon tah-ksee)

Shopping & Markets:

- Can I see that? – "¿Puedo ver eso?"
- (pweh-doh vehr eh-soh)

- What time do you open/close? – "¿A qué hora abren/cierran?"
- (ah keh oh-rah ah-bren / thyeh-ran)

- I'll take it – "Me lo llevo"
- (meh loh yeh-voh)

Polite Phrases:

- Please – "Por favor"
- (por fah-vohr)

- Thank you – "Gracias"
- (grah-thyahs)

- You're welcome – "De nada"
- (deh nah-dah)

- I'm sorry – "Lo siento"
- (loh syehn-toh)

Emergencies:

- Help! – "¡Ayuda!"
- (ah-yoo-dah)

- I need a doctor – "Necesito un médico"
- (neh-seh-see-toh oon meh-dee-koh)

- Call the police – "Llama a la policía"
- (yah-mah ah lah poh-lee-thee-ah)

When visiting Spain, having a basic understanding of the language is a great way to connect with locals and enrich your experience. It's always helpful to download a language app like Duolingo or Babbel, or carry a small Spanish phrasebook, which can guide you through common interactions and give you more confidence while traveling.

CHAPTER 4: MADRID

Neighborhood in Madrid

CHINCHÓN

Here's a detailed guide to the top accommodations, dining options, cafes, and nightlife in Chinchón, a charming town near Madrid, Spain:

TOP 3 LUXURY HOTELS IN CHINCHÓN

Parador de Chinchón

Set in a former Augustinian monastery, this elegant hotel offers stunning views of Chinchón's Plaza Mayor. The rooms are spacious, with a mix of traditional Spanish decor and modern comforts. The hotel also has a beautiful garden and outdoor pool.

Price: €150 - €250 per night

Address: Los Huertos, 1, 28370 Chinchón, Madrid, Spain

Hotel Condesa de Chinchón

A beautiful boutique hotel located near the Plaza Mayor. It offers charming rooms with traditional Spanish architecture, along with excellent service.

Price: €100 - €200 per night

Address: Calle de los Huertos, 26, 28370 Chinchón, Madrid, Spain

Terrazas a la Plaza

Located in a historic building with terraces overlooking Chinchón's central square, this luxury guesthouse offers spacious rooms with balconies, and it's perfect for those who want both comfort and great views.

Price: €120 - €220 per night

Address: Morata, 5, 28370 Chinchón, Madrid, Spain

TOP 4 MID-RANGE AND LOW BUDGET STAYS IN CHINCHÓN

La Casa Rural

A cozy, traditional guesthouse offering simple rooms and a warm atmosphere. Perfect for those looking for a budget-friendly and comfortable stay.

Price: €50 - €90 per night

Address: Calle Sociedad de Cosecheros, 5, 28370 Chinchón, Madrid, Spain

Hotel Rural Plaza Mayor

Located in the heart of Chinchón, this hotel offers mid-range rooms with classic decor and a relaxed atmosphere. It's perfect for a comfortable yet affordable stay.

Price: €60 - €110 per night

Address: Plaza Mayor, 38, 28370 Chinchón, Madrid, Spain

La Posada del Arco

A charming rural inn with simple yet well-appointed rooms, offering a great balance between comfort and budget. The location near the town center makes it convenient for sightseeing.

Price: €40 - €85 per night

Address: Calle del Arco, 28370 Chinchón, Madrid, Spain

Hostal Chinchón

A family-run guesthouse with basic but clean and affordable rooms. Ideal for budget-conscious travelers who want to stay close to the town center.

Price: €40 - €75 per night

Address: Calle de Morata, 9, 28370 Chinchón, Madrid, Spain

WHERE TO EAT IN CHINCHÓN

Mesón Cuevas del Vino

Known for its delicious roast lamb and cochinillo (suckling pig), this traditional restaurant offers local Castilian cuisine. The restaurant is set in a cave, providing a unique dining experience.

Address: Calle Sociedad de Cosecheros, 8, 28370 Chinchón, Madrid, Spain

Restaurante La Casa del Pregonero

A fine dining option offering a mix of traditional Spanish dishes with a modern twist. The food presentation and quality are excellent.

Address: Plaza Mayor, 17, 28370 Chinchón, Madrid, Spain

Restaurante La Balconada

Located in the Plaza Mayor, this restaurant specializes in local dishes like gazpacho and cocido madrileño. The restaurant's balcony offers great views of the town square.

Address: Plaza Mayor, 1, 28370 Chinchón, Madrid, Spain

COFFEE AND CAFÉ SHOPS IN CHINCHÓN

Café de la Iberia

Located near the Plaza Mayor, this charming café offers a wide range of coffees, pastries, and light snacks. The outdoor seating area is perfect for enjoying the atmosphere of the town.

Address: Calle Morata, 7, 28370 Chinchón, Madrid, Spain

Café La Villa

A small, cozy café known for its delicious churros and hot chocolate. It's a great place to relax after exploring the town.

Address: Calle Grande, 21, 28370 Chinchón, Madrid, Spain

El Rincón Del Chocolate

A must-visit for chocolate lovers, this café offers artisan hot chocolate, pastries, and local sweets. It's perfect for an afternoon treat.

Address: Plaza Mayor, 3, 28370 Chinchón, Madrid, Spain

BARS, NIGHTLIFE, AND ENTERTAINMENT IN CHINCHÓN

Bar Plaza Mayor

A lively bar located in the heart of the town, offering a great selection of Spanish wines, beers, and tapas. It's a great spot to start your evening.

Address: Plaza Mayor, 9, 28370 Chinchón, Madrid, Spain

La Taberna del Arriero

This traditional bar offers an authentic experience, with excellent local wines and tapas. The rustic atmosphere adds to its charm.

Address: Calle Sociedad de Cosecheros, 6, 28370 Chinchón, Madrid, Spain

La Casa del Marqués

A bar located in a historic building, offering cocktails and a more refined atmosphere. It's perfect for those looking for a quieter evening.

Address: Calle Morata, 13, 28370 Chinchón, Madrid, Spain

While Chinchón is a small town, it offers a wide range of accommodation options, delicious food, cozy cafés, and lively nightlife. Whether you're seeking luxury or a budget-friendly stay, you'll find something that suits your style.

SAN LORENZO DE EL ESCORIAL

Here's a comprehensive guide to top accommodations, dining options, cafes, and nightlife in San Lorenzo de El Escorial, a historic town known for its stunning royal monastery located near Madrid, Spain:

Top 2 Luxury Hotels in San Lorenzo de El Escorial

Hotel Los Lanceros

This elegant hotel combines modern comfort with traditional charm. It features spacious rooms and beautiful gardens, offering stunning views of the surrounding mountains.

Price: €120 - €220 per night

Address: Calle del Rey, 12, 28200 San Lorenzo de El Escorial, Madrid, Spain

Hotel Miranda & Suizo

This upscale hotel is located near the Monastery of El Escorial, featuring stylish rooms and an on-site restaurant that serves traditional Spanish cuisine. The ambiance is refined, perfect for a luxurious stay.

Price: €150 - €250 per night

Address: Avenida de la Reina Victoria, 1, 28200 San Lorenzo de El Escorial, Madrid, Spain

Top 3 Mid-Range and Low Budget Stays in San Lorenzo de El Escorial

Hotel Rural La Rasa

A charming rural hotel that offers a peaceful atmosphere with cozy accommodations. It's perfect for travelers looking for comfort without the luxury price tag.

Price: €60 - €100 per night

Address: Carretera M-600, Km 17, 28200 San Lorenzo de El Escorial, Madrid, Spain

Hostal Juan de Austria

This budget-friendly hostal provides clean and simple accommodations in a central location. It's ideal for travelers who want to explore San Lorenzo de El Escorial without overspending.

Price: €40 - €80 per night

Address: Calle Juan de Austria, 18, 28200 San Lorenzo de El Escorial, Madrid, Spain

Hotel El Escorial

Offering modern amenities and comfortable rooms, this hotel is well-situated for exploring the town and its historical sites. It's a good mid-range option.

Price: €70 - €120 per night

Address: Calle de la Huerta, 4, 28200 San Lorenzo de El Escorial, Madrid, Spain

Where to Eat in San Lorenzo de El Escorial

Restaurante El Escorial

Known for its delicious traditional Spanish dishes, this restaurant offers a cozy atmosphere and a varied menu, including local specialties.

Address: Calle Floridablanca, 10, 28200 San Lorenzo de El Escorial, Madrid, Spain

La Taberna de la Reina

A charming tavern that serves a variety of tapas and regional dishes. The rustic decor and friendly service make it a favorite among locals and visitors alike.

Address: Calle del Rey, 16, 28200 San Lorenzo de El Escorial, Madrid, Spain

El Cielo de Cobre

This trendy restaurant offers a mix of traditional and modern cuisine, focusing on fresh ingredients and innovative recipes. The ambiance is vibrant, making it perfect for a night out.

Address: Calle de la Huerta, 3, 28200 San Lorenzo de El Escorial, Madrid, Spain

Coffee and Café Shops in San Lorenzo de El Escorial

Café de la Villa

A cozy café known for its excellent coffee and pastries. It's a great spot to relax after a day of sightseeing or grab a light snack.

Address: Plaza de la Constitución, 1, 28200 San Lorenzo de El Escorial, Madrid, Spain

Cafetería La Parada

This local café offers a warm atmosphere, serving a variety of coffees, cakes, and light meals. It's perfect for a casual catch-up with friends.

Address: Calle de San Francisco, 10, 28200 San Lorenzo de El Escorial, Madrid, Spain

Bars, Nightlife, and Entertainment in San Lorenzo de El Escorial

Bar La Esquina

A lively bar offering a wide selection of drinks and tapas. It's a popular hangout spot for both locals and tourists, with a friendly atmosphere.

Address: Calle de la Reina, 5, 28200 San Lorenzo de El Escorial, Madrid, Spain

Pub La Juerga

A fun pub with live music and a vibrant nightlife scene. It's a great place to enjoy a night out with friends, featuring a variety of cocktails and beverages.

Address: Calle de Juan de Austria, 9, 28200 San Lorenzo de El Escorial, Madrid, Spain

Café Bar Tívoli

A popular café and bar that often hosts events and live music. The atmosphere is relaxed, making it a great spot to unwind after a busy day.

Address: Calle del Rey, 13, 28200 San Lorenzo de El Escorial, Madrid, Spain

San Lorenzo de El Escorial offers a rich blend of accommodations, dining experiences, cozy cafes, and lively nightlife, ensuring visitors have a memorable stay while exploring this historic town.

Museums and Galleries in Madrid

Madrid, Spain's capital, is a cultural hub known for its rich history, impressive art collections, and world-class museums and galleries. The city's museums house iconic works from Spain's most celebrated artists, including Picasso, Goya, Velázquez, and many others. In addition to art, the city has historical and archaeological museums that offer fascinating insights into Madrid's heritage.

1. Museo del Prado (Prado Museum)

Address: *Calle de Ruiz de Alarcón, 23, 28014 Madrid, Spain*

Entry Fee: €15 (General admission); Free from 6 PM to 8 PM (Monday to Saturday) and from 5 PM to 7 PM (Sundays and holidays)

The Prado Museum is one of the most famous art museums in the world and a must-see for visitors to Madrid. It houses an extensive collection of European art from the 12th to the early 20th century, with a particular focus on Spanish masters like Diego Velázquez, Francisco Goya, and El Greco. Iconic works include Velázquez's "Las Meninas", Goya's "The Third of May 1808", and Bosch's "The Garden of Earthly Delights".

2. Museo Nacional Centro de Arte Reina Sofía (Reina Sofía Museum)

Address: *Calle de Santa Isabel, 52, 28012 Madrid, Spain*

Entry Fee: €12 (General admission); Free from 7 PM to 9 PM (Monday to Saturday) and from 1:30 PM to 7 PM (Sundays)

The Reina Sofía Museum is Spain's national museum of 20th-century art. It is most famous for housing Pablo Picasso's "Guernica", a powerful anti-war painting that serves as a highlight of the museum. The collection also includes works by Salvador Dalí, Joan Miró, and other significant modern artists.

The museum also hosts rotating contemporary exhibitions and is located in an old hospital building with a stunning glass elevator.

3. Thyssen-Bornemisza Museum

Address: *Paseo del Prado, 8, 28014 Madrid, Spain*

Entry Fee: €13 (General admission); Free on Mondays from 12 PM to 4 PM

The Thyssen-Bornemisza Museum is part of Madrid's "Golden Triangle of Art" along with the Prado and Reina Sofía museums. It offers a broad collection of European paintings from the 13th to the 20th century, including works from the Italian Renaissance, Dutch Baroque, and 19th-century American art. Notable artists include Caravaggio, Rembrandt, Monet, Van Gogh, and Degas.

4. Museo Arqueológico Nacional (National Archaeological Museum)

Address: *Calle de Serrano, 13, 28001 Madrid, Spain*

Entry Fee: €3 (General admission); Free on Saturdays from 2 PM and Sundays

The National Archaeological Museum offers a deep dive into Spain's historical and cultural heritage, showcasing artifacts from prehistoric times through the 19th century. Its vast collection includes the famous "Lady of Elche" sculpture, ancient Roman mosaics, and Islamic art from the medieval period. The museum also features exhibitions on Egypt and ancient Greece, providing a broad historical context.

5. Museo Sorolla (Sorolla Museum)

Address: *Paseo del General Martínez Campos, 37, 28010 Madrid, Spain*

Entry Fee: €3 (General admission); Free on Saturdays from 2 PM and Sundays

Housed in the former home of the famous Spanish painter Joaquín Sorolla, this museum offers an intimate look at his life and work. Visitors can explore Sorolla's light-filled paintings, which often depict beaches, gardens, and family scenes. The museum also showcases Sorolla's personal art collection and includes a beautiful garden that he designed himself.

6. Museo Lázaro Galdiano

Address: *Calle de Serrano, 122, 28006 Madrid, Spain*

Entry Fee: €6 (General admission); Free on Sundays from 3 PM to 4:30 PM

The Lázaro Galdiano Museum is housed in the former mansion of the art collector José Lázaro Galdiano. Its collection spans a wide range of art periods and styles, with an emphasis on Spanish art. Noteworthy pieces include works by Goya, Zurbarán, and El Greco. The museum also features collections of decorative arts, including jewelry, textiles, and armor.

7. CaixaForum Madrid

Address: *Paseo del Prado, 36, 28014 Madrid, Spain*
Entry Fee: €6 (General admission); Prices vary for temporary exhibitions

CaixaForum Madrid is a contemporary art gallery housed in a strikingly modern building with a vertical garden. The gallery hosts a rotating series of exhibitions covering a wide range of artistic disciplines, from photography to painting to multimedia installations. It also hosts lectures, workshops, and performances, making it a vibrant cultural center in the city.

8. Real Academia de Bellas Artes de San Fernando

Address: *Calle de Alcalá, 13, 28014 Madrid, Spain*
Entry Fee: €8 (General admission)

This historic art academy and museum boasts a fine collection of paintings, sculptures, and prints dating from the 16th to the 20th century. Highlights include works by Goya, Zurbarán, and Sorolla. The museum is also notable for its architecture, with elegant galleries that reflect Madrid's artistic history.

9. Palacio de Cibeles (CentroCentro)

Address: *Plaza de Cibeles, 1, 28014 Madrid, Spain*
Entry Fee: Free for most exhibitions; €3 for the observation deck
Located in the iconic Palacio de Cibeles, this cultural center hosts a variety of exhibitions on modern art, photography, and design. Visitors can also take in panoramic views of Madrid from the observation deck, offering one of the best vantage points in the city.

Historical Sites in Madrid

1. Royal Palace of Madrid (Palacio Real)

Address: *Calle de Bailén, s/n, 28071 Madrid, Spain*
Entry Fee: €12 (General admission); Free for EU citizens from 5 PM to 7 PM (Monday to Thursday)
The Royal Palace of Madrid is the official residence of the Spanish royal family, though it is now used primarily for state

ceremonies. The palace is one of the largest in Europe and features 3,418 rooms, many of which are open to the public. Visitors can explore the grand Throne Room, the Royal Chapel, and the Royal Armory, which contains one of the most impressive collections of armor in the world. The palace also features stunning gardens, including the Campo del Moro and the Sabatini Gardens.

2. Plaza Mayor

Address: *Plaza Mayor, 28012 Madrid, Spain*

Entry Fee: Free

Plaza Mayor is a grand square in the heart of Madrid's historic district. Dating back to the 17th century, the square has been the site of markets, bullfights, and public celebrations. Today, it's a popular spot for tourists and locals alike, offering a range of cafes and shops. The central statue of King Philip III is a notable landmark, and the square's Baroque architecture is an iconic symbol of Madrid's history.

3. Puerta del Sol

Address: *Puerta del Sol, 28013 Madrid, Spain*

Entry Fee: Free

Puerta del Sol is one of Madrid's most famous landmarks and a central hub of the city. The square is home to several important monuments, including the "El Oso y El Madroño" (The Bear and the Strawberry Tree), the symbol of Madrid. It's also the location of Kilometer Zero, the point from which all distances in Spain are measured. Puerta del Sol is a lively place and a focal point for celebrations, including New Year's Eve.

4. Templo de Debod

Address: *Calle de Ferraz, 1, 28008 Madrid, Spain*

Entry Fee: Free

The Templo de Debod is an ancient Egyptian temple that was gifted to Spain in 1968 as a token of appreciation for Spain's help in saving the Abu Simbel temples in Egypt. The temple was reconstructed in Madrid's Parque del Oeste, offering visitors a unique glimpse into ancient Egyptian architecture. The surrounding park offers spectacular sunset views over the city.

5. El Retiro Park (Parque del Buen Retiro)

Address: *Plaza de la Independencia, 7, 28001 Madrid, Spain*

Entry Fee: Free

El Retiro Park is one of Madrid's largest and most popular parks, covering over 125 hectares. The park is a UNESCO World Heritage Site and offers a wide range of attractions, including the Crystal Palace, the Monument to Alfonso XII, and the Estanque Grande, a large lake where visitors can rent rowboats. The park is also home to the Parterre Garden, which contains Madrid's oldest tree, and various sculptures and fountains.

6. Almudena Cathedral (Catedral de la Almudena)

Address: *Calle de Bailén, 10, 28013 Madrid, Spain*

Entry Fee: €6 (includes entrance to the museum and the cathedral)

The Almudena Cathedral is Madrid's principal church, located next to the Royal Palace. Construction of the cathedral began in the late 19th century and was completed in 1993. The cathedral features a mix of architectural styles, including Neo-Gothic, Romanesque, and contemporary designs. Visitors can explore the crypt and take in panoramic views of Madrid from the dome.

7. San Francisco el Grande Basilica

Address: *Calle de San Buenaventura, 1, 28005 Madrid, Spain*

Entry Fee: €3 (General admission)

This Neoclassical basilica is known for its impressive dome, which is one of the largest in Spain. The interior is adorned with stunning frescoes and paintings by Goya, Zurbarán, and other notable Spanish artists. The basilica also has a small museum with religious artifacts and works of art.

These museums, galleries, and historical sites in Madrid provide a window into Spain's rich artistic, cultural, and historical heritage. From world-famous paintings to ancient temples and royal palaces, Madrid offers a wealth of experiences for visitors interested in exploring the past and present of this vibrant city.

Hiking in Madrid

Madrid offers excellent hiking opportunities with beautiful landscapes just outside the city, combining nature and history. From scenic mountains to tranquil forests, there are trails for all levels.

1. Sierra de Guadarrama National Park

Address: Carretera M-604, Km 27, 28470 Cercedilla, Madrid, Spain

Located just an hour away from Madrid, Sierra de Guadarrama National Park offers stunning mountain hikes, including the popular Siete Picos (Seven Peaks) and La Pedriza. The trails offer views of rugged peaks, rivers, and diverse flora and fauna.

2. Monte de El Pardo

Address: Monte de El Pardo, 28048 Madrid, Spain

Just a few kilometers from Madrid's city center, Monte de El Pardo is a large forested area ideal for easy walks and nature hikes. It's home to wildlife such as deer and birds, and offers peaceful hiking trails through Mediterranean woodlands.

3. La Pedriza

Address: Carretera M-608, Km 14, 28410 Manzanares el Real, Madrid, Spain

Situated in the Sierra de Guadarrama, La Pedriza is a rock formation known for its dramatic landscapes. It's popular among both hikers and climbers, offering routes that vary in difficulty, with panoramic views of the mountains.

4. Hayedo de Montejo

Address: Hayedo de Montejo, 28190 Montejo de la Sierra, Madrid, Spain

A beautiful beech forest located north of Madrid, perfect for an easy, scenic hike. This UNESCO-listed site is ideal for autumn hikes when the foliage turns vibrant.

Madrid's surrounding nature reserves and parks offer a blend of trails for casual hikers and experienced trekkers alike.

CHAPTER 5: BARCELONA

NEIGHBOURHOOD IN BARCELONA

SITGES

TOP 3 LUXURY HOTELS IN SITGES

Dolce by Wyndham Sitges Barcelona

Address: Av. Camí de Miralpeix, 12, 08870 Sitges, Barcelona, Spain

A stunning 5-star hotel with panoramic views of the Mediterranean, offering modern amenities, a wellness center, and excellent dining options.

Price: From €200 per night

Hotel MiM Sitges

Address: Av. Sofia, 12, 08870 Sitges, Barcelona, Spain

A chic luxury hotel designed by footballer Lionel Messi, featuring elegant rooms, a rooftop bar, a spa, and eco-friendly design.

Price: From €180 per night

ME Sitges Terramar

Address: Passeig Marítim, 80, 08870 Sitges, Barcelona, Spain

A luxury beachfront hotel offering sleek, contemporary rooms, a rooftop lounge, and direct access to the beach.

Price: From €220 per night

TOP 4 MID-RANGE AND LOW-BUDGET STAYS

Hotel Medium Sitges Park

Address: Carrer Jesús, 16, 08870 Sitges, Barcelona, Spain

A charming 3-star hotel with a garden, outdoor pool, and modern rooms in a historic building.

Price: From €90 per night

Hotel Galeón

Address: Carrer de Sant Francesc, 44, 08870 Sitges, Barcelona, Spain

A mid-range hotel offering comfortable rooms, a pool, and an excellent breakfast.

Price: From €80 per night

Hotel Capri

Address: Av. Sofia, 13, 08870 Sitges, Barcelona, Spain

A cozy family-run hotel with beautiful gardens, a pool, and a relaxed atmosphere close to the beach.

Price: From €75 per night

Hostal Termes

Address: Carrer d'Enric Morera, 2, 08870 Sitges, Barcelona, Spain

A budget-friendly hostel offering clean, comfortable rooms with a convenient location near the beach.

Price: From €60 per night

WHERE TO EAT IN SITGES

Casa Hidalgo

Address: Carrer Bonaire, 18, 08870 Sitges, Barcelona, Spain

A traditional Spanish restaurant known for its tapas, seafood, and paella.

La Zorra

Address: Passeig de la Ribera, 30, 08870 Sitges, Barcelona, Spain

A trendy restaurant specializing in creative paellas and local cuisine with Mediterranean flavors.

El Trull

Address: Carrer de l'Aigua, 9, 08870 Sitges, Barcelona, Spain

A cozy, romantic spot serving a blend of Catalan and Mediterranean dishes.

COFFEE AND CAFÉ SHOPS IN SITGES

Café Roy

Address: Carrer de Sant Pau, 11, 08870 Sitges, Barcelona, Spain

A lovely café offering great coffee, pastries, and light snacks in a relaxed environment.

La Sitgetana Craftbeer Café

Address: Carrer de Sant Bartomeu, 10, 08870 Sitges, Barcelona, Spain

A cozy café and brewery with artisanal beers, coffee, and light bites.

Café de la Plata

Address: Passeig de la Ribera, 12, 08870 Sitges, Barcelona, Spain

A beachfront café offering espresso, cakes, and snacks with a stunning sea view.

BARS, NIGHTLIFE, AND ENTERTAINMENT
El Gin Tub

Address: Carrer de Bonaire, 16, 08870 Sitges, Barcelona, Spain

A lively gin bar with an extensive selection of craft gins and creative cocktails.

La Villa

Address: Carrer Primer de Maig, 5, 08870 Sitges, Barcelona, Spain

A stylish lounge bar offering excellent cocktails and a chic setting.

Queenz Cabaret Restaurant

Address: Carrer Bonaire, 17, 08870 Sitges, Barcelona, Spain

A fun spot combining cabaret shows and a vibrant nightlife experience.

CADAQUÉS

Top 3 Luxury Hotels in Cadaqués

Hotel Playa Sol

Address: Riba es Pianc, 3, 17488 Cadaqués, Girona, Spain

A beachfront hotel offering stunning sea views, elegant rooms, and an outdoor pool. It's known for its relaxing ambiance and modern amenities.

Price: From €200 per night

Boutique Hotel Villa Gala

Address: Carrer Solitari, 3, 17488 Cadaqués, Girona, Spain

A chic boutique hotel offering luxurious rooms with a mix of modern design and Mediterranean flair. It features a pool and garden terrace with beautiful views of Cadaqués.

Price: From €240 per night

Hotel Tramuntana

Address: Carrer Sa Tarongeta, 1, 17488 Cadaqués, Girona, Spain

A refined hotel with contemporary decor, offering an intimate, quiet setting. Guests appreciate the exceptional service and cozy, stylish rooms.

Price: From €220 per night

Top 4 Mid-Range and Low-Budget Stays in Cadaqués

Hotel Blaumar

Address: Riera de Sant Vicenç, s/n, 17488 Cadaqués, Girona, Spain

A mid-range hotel with comfortable rooms, an outdoor pool, and close proximity to the beach.

Price: From €110 per night

Hostal Marina

Address: Riera Sant Vicenç, 5, 17488 Cadaqués, Girona, Spain

A charming and affordable guesthouse in the heart of Cadaqués, offering basic rooms and a family-friendly atmosphere.

Price: From €70 per night

Hotel Octavia

Address: Riera de Sant Vicenç, s/n, 17488 Cadaqués, Girona, Spain

A budget-friendly option with clean, spacious rooms and excellent location near the town center and beach.

Price: From €90 per night

L'Hostalet de Cadaqués

Address: Carrer Miquel Rosset, 13, 17488 Cadaqués, Girona, Spain

A simple, affordable stay offering cozy rooms with easy access to the beach and local attractions.

Price: From €65 per night

Where to Eat in Cadaqués

Compartir

Address: Riera de Sant Vicenç, 17488 Cadaqués, Girona, Spain

Offers innovative Catalan cuisine, perfect for sharing dishes with family or friends.

Specialty: Mediterranean and seafood dishes.

Can Rafa

Address: Riba Nemesi Llorens, 17, 17488 Cadaqués, Girona, Spain

Famous for its fresh seafood and traditional Catalan dishes, located near the waterfront.

Talla

Address: Carrer de l'Esculapi, 8, 17488 Cadaqués, Girona, Spain
A seafood restaurant with spectacular views and a relaxing atmosphere, offering high-quality dishes.

Coffee and Café Shops

Café de la Habana

Address: Carrer des Pla de Portlligat, 17488 Cadaqués, Girona, Spain
A cozy café with great coffee, pastries, and a chilled-out vibe.

Pastisseria La Mallorquina

Address: Carrer Miquel Rosset, 6, 17488 Cadaqués, Girona, Spain
A local bakery and café offering delicious pastries, coffee, and light bites.

Bar Boia Nit

Address: Passeig Marítim, 15, 17488 Cadaqués, Girona, Spain
A popular spot for coffee during the day and cocktails by night, right by the sea.

Bars, Nightlife, and Entertainment

Boia Nit

Address: Passeig Marítim, 15, 17488 Cadaqués, Girona, Spain

One of the most famous bars in Cadaqués, offering a mix of signature cocktails and stunning seaside views.

Bar Mut

Address: Carrer Nou, 12, 17488 Cadaqués, Girona, Spain

A lively spot for drinks and socializing, popular with locals and tourists alike.

Marítim Bar

Address: Passeig Marítim, 5, 17488 Cadaqués, Girona, Spain

A chill beach bar with a laid-back atmosphere, ideal for sunset drinks and live music.

Cadaqués offers a blend of upscale and budget-friendly options with plenty of places to eat, relax, and enjoy the vibrant nightlife.

Museums and Galleries in Barcelona

Museu Picasso

Address: Carrer Montcada, 15-23, 08003 Barcelona

Entry Fee: €12 (permanent collection), €7 (temporary exhibitions)

The Picasso Museum houses one of the most extensive collections of the artist's early works, making it one of the most visited museums in Barcelona. Set in five medieval palaces, the museum focuses on Picasso's formative years and his close connection to Barcelona. It also hosts temporary exhibitions of modern art.

Fundació Joan Miró

Address: *Parc de Montjuïc, 08038 Barcelona*

Entry Fee: €14 (general admission), free on certain days for residents

The Joan Miró Foundation showcases a wide collection of the Catalan artist's works, ranging from paintings and sculptures to drawings and early sketches. The foundation also hosts temporary exhibits and offers stunning views over Barcelona from its location on Montjuïc Hill.

Museu Nacional d'Art de Catalunya (MNAC)

Address: *Palau Nacional, Parc de Montjuïc, 08038 Barcelona*

Entry Fee: €12 (general admission), free on the first Sunday of each month

MNAC is one of the most important museums in Spain, displaying Catalan art from the Romanesque period through to the 20th century. The museum is housed in the Palau Nacional, a grand building that was originally constructed for the 1929 International Exhibition.

MACBA (Museu d'Art Contemporani de Barcelona)

Address: Plaça dels Àngels, 1, 08001 Barcelona

Entry Fee: €11 (general admission)

The Barcelona Museum of Contemporary Art (MACBA) focuses on post-1945 Catalan and Spanish art, showcasing works in various media including painting, video art, and performance. The museum is renowned for its sleek, modern architecture, designed by Richard Meier.

Museu d'Història de Barcelona (MUHBA)

Address: Plaça del Rei, s/n, 08002 Barcelona

Entry Fee: €7 (general admission)

MUHBA is dedicated to the history of Barcelona, with exhibits stretching from Roman times to the modern day. Visitors can explore underground Roman ruins and get a detailed look at the development of the city. The museum also operates several satellite sites across the city.

Museu del Modernisme de Barcelona

Address: Carrer de Balmes, 48, 08007 Barcelona

Entry Fee: €10 (general admission)

This museum is dedicated to the Catalan modernist movement and showcases works from famous artists and architects such as Antoni Gaudí and Ramon Casas. Housed in a beautifully restored modernist building, it offers visitors a chance to dive into Barcelona's architectural heritage.

Fundació Antoni Tàpies

Address: Carrer d'Aragó, 255, 08007 Barcelona

Entry Fee: €8 (general admission)

Dedicated to the work of one of Spain's most significant contemporary artists, Antoni Tàpies, the foundation houses a collection of his paintings, sculptures, and installations. The building itself is an architectural masterpiece designed by Domènech i Montaner, a key figure in Catalan modernism.

Museu Frederic Marès

Address: Plaça de Sant Iu, 5, 08002 Barcelona

Entry Fee: €4.20 (general admission)

This museum houses an eclectic collection of sculptures, religious artifacts, and everyday items from various periods, all collected by sculptor Frederic Marès. It's located in the Gothic Quarter, making it a great stop while exploring the historical heart of Barcelona.

Historical Sites in Barcelona:

La Sagrada Família

Address: Carrer de Mallorca, 401, 08013 Barcelona

Entry Fee: €26 (basic admission)

Antoni Gaudí's unfinished basilica is perhaps the most iconic building in Barcelona. Construction began in 1882 and continues to this day. Visitors can marvel at the intricate details of the basilica's facades, stained-glass windows, and unique architectural elements influenced by natural forms.

Park Güell

Address: Carrer d'Olot, s/n, 08024 Barcelona

Entry Fee: €10 (general admission)

Another of Gaudí's masterpieces, Park Güell is a surreal landscape of twisting pathways, colorful mosaics, and organic forms. Located on Carmel Hill, the park offers panoramic views of the city and is a UNESCO World Heritage site. It is a must-visit for architecture lovers.

La Pedrera (Casa Milà)

Address: Passeig de Gràcia, 92, 08008 Barcelona

Entry Fee: €24 (general admission)

Casa Milà, also known as La Pedrera, is another of Gaudí's groundbreaking designs. The undulating façade and unique rooftop sculptures make it one of the most famous modernist buildings in the world. Inside, visitors can tour apartments and exhibition spaces dedicated to Gaudí's work.

Casa Batlló

Address: Passeig de Gràcia, 43, 08007 Barcelona

Entry Fee: €35 (general admission)

Casa Batlló is yet another of Gaudí's iconic creations, known for its striking façade that resembles dragon scales. The interior is equally impressive, with flowing lines, colorful tile work, and a skylight that mimics the shape of a tortoise shell.

Barcelona Cathedral

Address: Pla de la Seu, s/n, 08002 Barcelona

Entry Fee: €9 (general admission)

Located in the Gothic Quarter, Barcelona Cathedral (also known as the Cathedral of the Holy Cross and Saint Eulalia) is an impressive example of Gothic architecture. Visitors can explore the interior, cloister, and rooftop, which offers stunning views of the city.

Palau de la Música Catalana

Address: Carrer Palau de la Música, 4-6, 08003 Barcelona

Entry Fee: €20 (guided tour)

A UNESCO World Heritage site, the Palau de la Música Catalana is a modernist concert hall designed by Lluís Domènech i Montaner. Its stunning stained-glass ceiling and lavish decoration make it one of Barcelona's most beautiful buildings. Guided tours are available for those who want to learn more about its history and architecture.

Montjuïc Castle

Address: Ctra. de Montjuïc, 66, 08038 Barcelona

Entry Fee: €5 (general admission), free on Sundays after 3 pm

Montjuïc Castle sits atop Montjuïc Hill and has played a significant role in Barcelona's history, particularly during times of war. The castle offers spectacular views of the city and the sea. It also hosts cultural events and exhibitions.

Plaça Reial

Address: Plaça Reial, 08002 Barcelona

Entry Fee: Free

Located near La Rambla, Plaça Reial is a beautiful square lined with palm trees and impressive arcades. It's home to several restaurants, cafes, and bars, making it a lively spot for both locals and tourists. In the center of the square is the Fountain of the Three Graces, surrounded by lampposts designed by Gaudí.

Parks and Gardens in Barcelona

Parc de la Ciutadella

Address: Passeig de Picasso, 21, 08003 Barcelona

Entry Fee: Free

Parc de la Ciutadella is one of the largest green spaces in Barcelona, offering a peaceful retreat from the city's hustle and bustle. The park features a large fountain designed by Gaudí, a boating lake, and several museums, including the Barcelona Zoo and the Museu de Geologia.

Jardins de Joan Brossa

Address: Plaça Dante, 08038 Barcelona

Entry Fee: Free

Located on Montjuïc Hill, these gardens offer a mix of art and nature, with sculptures scattered among the greenery. It's a great spot for a leisurely walk while taking in views of the city below.

Parc del Laberint d'Horta

Address: Passeig dels Castanyers, 1, 08035 Barcelona

Entry Fee: €2.23 (general admission), free on Sundays

The Parc del Laberint d'Horta is a hidden gem in Barcelona, known for its lush greenery and charming labyrinth made of cypress hedges. The park is perfect for a quiet afternoon and offers a unique escape into nature.

From museums that house works of iconic artists to historical landmarks like La Sagrada Família and Park Güell, the city is a must-visit for culture enthusiasts. Whether you're exploring its museums, admiring modernist buildings, or relaxing in its parks, Barcelona offers a rich and immersive cultural experience.

CHAPTER 6: VALENCIA

CHULILLA

Top 3 Luxury Hotels in Chulilla

Hotel La Masía

Address: Calle del Limonero, 5, 46166 Chulilla, Valencia, Spain
Price: Approximately €120-€180 per night
A charming hotel featuring modern amenities, an outdoor pool, and beautiful views of the surrounding countryside.

Hotel Rural El Vino

Address: Calle del Vino, 16, 46166 Chulilla, Valencia, Spain
Price: Approximately €100-€150 per night
This hotel combines rustic charm with modern comfort, offering a cozy atmosphere and excellent service.

Casa Rural La Pina

Address: Carrer de la Font, 4, 46166 Chulilla, Valencia, Spain
Price: Approximately €90-€150 per night

A rural hotel with comfortable accommodations, a garden, and a terrace with stunning views.

Top 4 Mid-Range and Low-Budget Stays in Chulilla

Hostal Rural El Pinar
Address: Calle de la Cuesta, 9, 46166 Chulilla, Valencia, Spain
Price: Approximately €50-€80 per night
A cozy hostal offering comfortable rooms and easy access to outdoor activities.

Alojamientos Rurales Chulilla
Address: Calle San José, 15, 46166 Chulilla, Valencia, Spain
Price: Approximately €60-€90 per night
A rustic guesthouse with a friendly atmosphere, providing a great base for exploring the area.

Casa Rural La Cueva
Address: Calle de la Luz, 1, 46166 Chulilla, Valencia, Spain
Price: Approximately €70-€100 per night

A charming rural house with basic amenities and a welcoming ambiance.

Pensión Casa Evaristo

Address: Calle de San Pedro, 7, 46166 Chulilla, Valencia, Spain
Price: Approximately €40-€70 per night
An affordable guesthouse with simple accommodations, ideal for budget travelers.

Where to Eat in Chulilla

Restaurante El Rincón

Address: Calle del Barco, 5, 46166 Chulilla, Valencia, Spain
A local restaurant known for its delicious paella and traditional Spanish dishes.

Restaurante La Tertulia

Address: Calle de la Llum, 2, 46166 Chulilla, Valencia, Spain
Offers a variety of Mediterranean cuisine with fresh, local ingredients.

Bar Restaurante La Parra

Address: Calle del Puente, 8, 46166 Chulilla, Valencia, Spain
A casual dining spot with tapas, local wines, and friendly service.
Coffee and Café Shops in Chulilla

Cafetería Chulilla

Address: Calle de la Huerta, 10, 46166 Chulilla, Valencia, Spain
A cozy café serving breakfast, pastries, and great coffee.

Bar Cafetería El Camino

Address: Calle de la Playa, 4, 46166 Chulilla, Valencia, Spain
A popular spot for coffee, snacks, and light meals in a friendly atmosphere.

Bars, Nightlife, and Entertainment in Chulilla

Bar La Plaza

Address: Plaza de la Iglesia, 3, 46166 Chulilla, Valencia, Spain
A lively bar offering drinks, tapas, and a great atmosphere for socializing.

Bar Restaurante La Cueva

Address: Calle de la Cueva, 2, 46166 Chulilla, Valencia, Spain
A bar and restaurant that hosts occasional live music and events.

Cafetería Bar La Almazara

Address: Calle de la Almazara, 1, 46166 Chulilla, Valencia, Spain
A relaxed bar with a variety of beverages and light meals, perfect for unwinding after a day of exploring.
Chulilla offers a mix of accommodations, dining options, and entertainment to ensure a pleasant stay for all visitors.

ALTEA

Top 3 Luxury Hotels in Altea

Hotel Cap Negret

Address: Partida Cap Negret, 2, 03590 Altea, Alicante, Spain
Price: Approximately €150-€250 per night
A beachfront hotel offering stunning sea views, luxurious amenities, and an outdoor pool.

Sh Villa Gadea

Address: Av. de la Villa Gadea, 1, 03590 Altea, Alicante, Spain

Price: Approximately €200-€300 per night

A 5-star hotel with elegant rooms, a spa, multiple pools, and beautiful gardens.

Hotel La Serena

Address: Calle de la Reina Sofía, 15, 03590 Altea, Alicante, Spain

Price: Approximately €120-€180 per night

A boutique hotel featuring modern décor, an outdoor pool, and proximity to the beach.

Top 4 Mid-Range and Low-Budget Stays in Altea

Hotel Noguera

Address: Calle de la Noguera, 1, 03590 Altea, Alicante, Spain

Price: Approximately €60-€100 per night

A comfortable hotel with a friendly atmosphere, offering basic amenities and easy access to the beach.

Hostal El Trovador

Address: Calle del Trovador, 3, 03590 Altea, Alicante, Spain
Price: Approximately €50-€80 per night
A budget-friendly option with simple rooms and a great location in the town center.

Pensión Los Almendros

Address: Calle de la Almendra, 4, 03590 Altea, Alicante, Spain
Price: Approximately €40-€70 per night
A cozy guesthouse offering comfortable accommodations at an affordable price.

Camping Altea

Address: Partida de la Torre, 9, 03590 Altea, Alicante, Spain
Price: Approximately €30-€50 per night (for camping)
An excellent budget option for nature lovers, offering camping facilities near the beach.

Where to Eat in Altea

Restaurante Oustau

Address: Carrer de la Mar, 1, 03590 Altea, Alicante, Spain
A Mediterranean restaurant specializing in fresh seafood and local dishes.

Casa del Maco

Address: Av. del Albir, 1, 03590 Altea, Alicante, Spain

Known for its delicious Mediterranean cuisine and beautiful sea views.

La Cova

Address: Calle del Cava, 8, 03590 Altea, Alicante, Spain

A charming spot offering tapa, local wines, and a cozy atmosphere.

Coffee and Café Shops in Altea

Café de Paris

Address: Av. de la Marina, 1, 03590 Altea, Alicante, Spain

A popular café serving coffee, pastries, and breakfast options in a charming setting.

Café 3

Address: Calle del Mar, 12, 03590 Altea, Alicante, Spain

A cozy spot to enjoy coffee, snacks, and light meals, perfect for relaxing.

Bars, Nightlife, and Entertainment in Altea

Bar La Fonda

Address: Calle de la Iglesia, 2, 03590 Altea, Alicante, Spain

A lively bar known for its cocktails and friendly atmosphere.

Bar El Canto

Address: Calle del Canto, 4, 03590 Altea, Alicante, Spain

A popular spot for tapas and drinks, often featuring live music.

Café Bar Noa

Address: Av. de la Marina, 3, 03590 Altea, Alicante, Spain

A relaxed bar offering a variety of beverages and snacks, great for socializing after a day of exploring.

Altea has a diverse selection of accommodations, dining options, and nightlife to cater to various preferences and budgets, ensuring a delightful experience for all visitors.

Museums and Galleries in Valencia

Valencia, a city known for its stunning architecture and rich history, is home to several prominent museums and galleries.

Each one offers a unique perspective on the city's art, culture, and historical heritage.

1. Museu de Belles Arts de València

Address: Calle San Pío V, 9, 46010 Valencia

Entry Fee: Free

The Museum of Fine Arts is one of Spain's most significant art galleries, featuring an impressive collection of paintings from the Gothic period to the 20th century. Visitors can enjoy works by renowned artists like Diego Velázquez, El Greco, and Francisco de Goya. The museum is set in a beautiful baroque building and is surrounded by tranquil gardens.

2. Institut Valencià d'Art Modern (IVAM)

Address: Guillem de Castro, 118, 46003 Valencia

Entry Fee: €6 (general admission), free on Sundays

The Valencia Institute of Modern Art (IVAM) is dedicated to contemporary art, with a particular focus on 20th-century artists. It offers a mix of permanent and temporary exhibitions, including works by Spanish and international artists. The museum also organizes cultural events and workshops, making it a dynamic part of Valencia's art scene.

3. Museo de la Ciudad

Address: Plaza del Arzobispo, 3, 46003 Valencia

Entry Fee: €2 (general admission)

The City Museum provides a comprehensive look at Valencia's history through its collection of archaeological artifacts, sculptures, and paintings. It is housed in the 18th-century Palacio de Cervelló and offers visitors insight into the city's transformation over the centuries, from its Roman origins to its modern-day status as a cultural hub.

4. Museo Nacional de Cerámica y Artes Suntuarias González Martí

Address: Calle del Poeta Querol, 2, 46002 Valencia

Entry Fee: €3 (general admission), free on Saturdays after 4 pm and Sundays

Housed in the stunning Palace of the Marqués de Dos Aguas, the National Museum of Ceramics features an extensive collection of Spanish ceramics, including pieces from Valencia's own traditional production. The museum also displays furniture, clothing, and other decorative arts from various periods.

5. Museo de Historia de Valencia

Address: Calle Valencia a Ademuz, 46035 Valencia

Entry Fee: €2 (general admission)

The Museum of the History of Valencia takes visitors on a journey through the city's past, showcasing its evolution from a Roman colony to a modern metropolis. The museum's interactive displays, audiovisual exhibits, and historical objects provide an engaging experience for all ages.

6. Centre del Carme Cultura Contemporània

Address: Calle del Museu, 2, 46003 Valencia

Entry Fee: Free

Located in a former convent, the Centre del Carme is now a thriving cultural space that hosts contemporary art exhibitions, performances, and workshops. The building itself is a work of art, with Gothic and Renaissance elements, and visitors can explore the cloisters and gardens while enjoying the exhibitions.

Historical Sites in Valencia

Valencia's rich history is reflected in its many well-preserved historical sites, from ancient towers to magnificent cathedrals.

1. La Lonja de la Seda (Silk Exchange)

Address: Plaza del Mercado, 46001 Valencia

Entry Fee: €2 (general admission), free on Sundays and holidays

A UNESCO World Heritage site, La Lonja de la Seda is a stunning example of late Gothic architecture. Built in the 15th century, it served as a marketplace for silk traders and is renowned for its elaborate stone carvings and stunning vaulted ceilings. The interior hall, known as the Sala de Contratación, is particularly impressive, with its towering columns and ribbed vaults.

2. Valencia Cathedral

Address: Plaza de la Reina, s/n, 46003 Valencia

Entry Fee: €8 (general admission)

The Valencia Cathedral, also known as the Metropolitan Cathedral-Basilica of the Assumption of Our Lady of Valencia, is a blend of Gothic, Romanesque, and Baroque styles. It is home to what is believed to be the Holy Grail, the chalice used by Jesus during the Last Supper. Visitors can also climb the cathedral's Miguelete Tower for panoramic views of the city.

3. Torres de Serranos

Address: Plaza de los Fueros, s/n, 46003 Valencia

Entry Fee: €2 (general admission), free on Sundays

The Serranos Towers were built in the 14th century as part of Valencia's city walls. Today, they stand as one of the best-preserved Gothic military structures in Europe. Visitors can explore the towers and enjoy spectacular views of the old city from the top.

4. Torres de Quart

Address: Calle Guillem de Castro, 89, 46003 Valencia

Entry Fee: €2 (general admission), free on Sundays

Similar to the Serranos Towers, the Quart Towers were part of Valencia's medieval fortifications. Built in the 15th century, they bear the scars of past battles, including cannonball damage from the Napoleonic Wars. Visitors can climb the towers for another fantastic viewpoint of the city.

5. Plaza de la Virgen

Address: Plaza de la Virgen, 46001 Valencia

Entry Fee: Free

One of the most picturesque squares in Valencia, Plaza de la Virgen is surrounded by historical buildings such as the Valencia Cathedral, the Basílica de la Virgen de los Desamparados, and the Palau de la Generalitat. It's a popular spot for locals and tourists alike, offering a peaceful atmosphere with its central fountain and beautiful architecture.

6. Almoina Archaeological Center

Address: Plaza Decimo Junio Bruto, s/n, 46003 Valencia

Entry Fee: €2 (general admission)

The Almoina Archaeological Center provides a glimpse into Valencia's Roman past, with excavated ruins that date back over 2,000 years. Visitors can explore the remains of ancient baths, streets, and buildings, as well as artifacts from Roman, Visigoth, and Islamic periods.

Parks and Gardens in Valencia

1. Jardín del Turia

Address: Turia Riverbed, 46010 Valencia

Entry Fee: Free

One of the largest urban parks in Spain, the Turia Gardens stretch for nine kilometers along the former course of the Turia River. The park is a green oasis in the heart of the city, offering walking and cycling paths, fountains, and playgrounds. It's also home to several cultural attractions, including the City of Arts and Sciences.

2. Jardines del Real (Viveros)

Address: Calle de San Pío V, 46010 Valencia

Entry Fee: Free

The Royal Gardens, also known as Viveros, are one of Valencia's most beautiful green spaces. Once the site of a royal palace, the gardens are now a peaceful retreat filled with statues, fountains, and a wide variety of plant species. It's an ideal spot for a leisurely stroll or a picnic.

3. L'Albufera Natural Park

Address: El Saler, 46012 Valencia

Entry Fee: Free, boat tours cost extra

Located just outside the city, L'Albufera Natural Park is a vast wetland area that is home to a rich variety of wildlife, including many species of birds. The park's large freshwater lagoon is perfect for boat tours, and the surrounding rice fields provide the main ingredient for Valencia's famous paella.

With a variety of entry options and plenty of free attractions, the city is accessible to all kinds of travelers.

CHAPTER 7: SEVILLE

ALCALÁ DE GUADAÍRA

Top 3 Luxury Hotels in Alcalá de Guadaíra

Hotel Oromana

Address: Avenida Portugal, s/n, 41500 Alcalá de Guadaíra, Seville, Spain

Price: Starting from €140 per night

A historical hotel with Andalusian charm, offering luxury amenities, spacious rooms, and stunning views of the Oromana Pine Forest and the Guadaíra River.

Hacienda de Orán

Address: Autovia Sevilla-Utrera, Km. 13.5, 41710 Utrera, Seville, Spain

Price: Starting from €180 per night

A 17th-century estate transformed into a luxury rural retreat, featuring elegant suites, an outdoor pool, and extensive gardens.

Hotel Silken Al-Andalus Palace

Address: Avenida de la Palmera, s/n, 41012 Seville, Spain (20-minute drive from Alcalá de Guadaíra)
Price: Starting from €160 per night
A contemporary luxury hotel with modern design, boasting lush gardens, a large pool, and fine dining options.

Top 4 Mid-Range and Low Budget Stays
Hotel Sandra
Address: Calle Mairena, 6, 41500 Alcalá de Guadaíra, Seville, Spain
Price: Starting from €60 per night
A comfortable hotel with basic amenities, located in the town center and offering easy access to local attractions.

Hostal Nueva Andalucía
Address: Calle el Álamo, 2, 41500 Alcalá de Guadaíra, Seville, Spain
Price: Starting from €45 per night
A budget-friendly guesthouse providing clean, simple rooms with private bathrooms and free parking.

Hostal San Francisco

Address: Calle San Francisco, 15, 41500 Alcalá de Guadaíra, Seville, Spain

Price: Starting from €50 per night

A charming, budget accommodation offering cozy rooms and a traditional Andalusian courtyard.

Hotel Guadaíra

Address: Calle Mairena, 8, 41500 Alcalá de Guadaíra, Seville, Spain

Price: Starting from €55 per night

A simple, affordable hotel close to the river, with spacious rooms and excellent customer service.

Where to Eat

Restaurante La Taberna del Sarmiento

Address: Calle Madueño de los Aires, 9, 41500 Alcalá de Guadaíra, Seville, Spain

A rustic restaurant specializing in traditional Andalusian dishes, including tapas, seafood, and meat dishes.

Mesón La Doma

Address: Calle Escultor Duque Cornejo, 8, 41500 Alcalá de Guadaíra, Seville, Spain

A family-run eatery offering local cuisine with a focus on grilled meats and homemade desserts.

Casa Rufino

Address: Avenida Tren de los Panaderos, 12, 41500 Alcalá de Guadaíra, Seville, Spain

Known for its seafood dishes, this restaurant is popular among locals for its authentic flavor and quality.

Coffee and Café Shops

Café Bar La Esquina

Address: Calle Sanlúcar la Mayor, 2, 41500 Alcalá de Guadaíra, Seville, Spain

A local favorite for coffee, breakfast, and pastries.

Café de Indias

Address: Avenida de Portugal, s/n, 41500 Alcalá de Guadaíra, Seville, Spain

A popular café chain offering a wide range of coffee options, teas, and light snacks.

La Antigua Cafetería

Address: Plaza del Perejil, 4, 41500 Alcalá de Guadaíra, Seville, Spain

A cozy spot for a casual coffee with homemade pastries and sandwiches.

Bars, Nightlife, and Entertainment
Bar El Palenque

Address: Calle General Prim, 5, 41500 Alcalá de Guadaíra, Seville, Spain

A lively local bar offering affordable drinks, tapas, and occasional live music.

Pub Dublín

Address: Calle Álamo, 10, 41500 Alcalá de Guadaíra, Seville, Spain

An Irish-style pub, perfect for enjoying a drink with friends in a laid-back atmosphere.

La Terraza de Oromana

Address: Avenida Portugal, s/n, 41500 Alcalá de Guadaíra, Seville, Spain

A rooftop terrace bar located at Hotel Oromana, offering stunning views and a refined setting for cocktails and evening relaxation.

Alcalá de Guadaíra offers a variety of accommodations and entertainment for all types of travelers, from luxurious stays to budget-friendly options, along with diverse dining and nightlife options to suit any preference.

CARMONA

Top 3 Luxury Hotels in Carmona

Parador de Carmona

Address: Carretera de la Esquina, s/n, 41410 Carmona, Seville, Spain
Price: Starting from €140 per night
A historic hotel located in a former castle, offering stunning views, elegant rooms, and a beautiful outdoor pool.

Hotel Casa de Carmona

Address: Calle San José, 10, 41410 Carmona, Seville, Spain

Price: Starting from €160 per night

A luxurious boutique hotel set in a 16th-century mansion, featuring charming rooms, lush gardens, and an outdoor pool.

Hotel Los Cántaros

Address: Av. de la Libertad, 15, 41410 Carmona, Seville, Spain

Price: Starting from €120 per night

A stylish hotel with modern amenities, a restaurant, and a lovely terrace overlooking the historic town.

Top 4 Mid-Range and Low Budget Stays

Hotel Alcázar de la Reina

Address: Calle Carlos de Guzmán, 4, 41410 Carmona, Seville, Spain

Price: Starting from €80 per night

A comfortable hotel with traditional Andalusian decor, featuring cozy rooms and easy access to local attractions.

Hotel Casa de la Condesa

Address: Calle José de la Campa, 7, 41410 Carmona, Seville, Spain

Price: Starting from €70 per night

A charming guesthouse located in the town center, offering clean rooms and friendly service.

Hostal La Campana

Address: Calle La Campana, 14, 41410 Carmona, Seville, Spain
Price: Starting from €50 per night
A budget-friendly hostal providing basic accommodations with a central location, ideal for exploring Carmona.

Hotel El Mirador

Address: Av. de la Constitución, 8, 41410 Carmona, Seville, Spain
Price: Starting from €60 per night
A quaint hotel with simple yet comfortable rooms, located close to historical sites and restaurants.

Where to Eat

Restaurante La Cazuela
Address: Calle Ronda de la Pza., 6, 41410 Carmona, Seville, Spain
A traditional Spanish restaurant known for its delicious tapas and local dishes, served in a warm, inviting atmosphere.

Mesón La Villa

Address: Calle Juan Carlos I, 13, 41410 Carmona, Seville, Spain

A popular eatery specializing in grilled meats and Andalusian cuisine, offering generous portions and a friendly vibe.

Restaurante La Huerta

Address: Calle José de la Campa, 6, 41410 Carmona, Seville, Spain

A cozy restaurant with a lovely terrace, serving a range of Mediterranean dishes and vegetarian options.

Coffee and Café Shops

Café Bar La Plaza

Address: Plaza de San Fernando, 8, 41410 Carmona, Seville, Spain

A charming café perfect for enjoying coffee, pastries, and light snacks while taking in the local atmosphere.

Café La Novena

Address: Calle Alhóndiga, 3, 41410 Carmona, Seville, Spain

A cozy coffee shop offering a variety of coffee drinks, homemade cakes, and breakfast options.

Bar Café La Calle

Address: Calle San José, 1, 41410 Carmona, Seville, Spain

A popular spot for locals, serving good coffee and traditional tapas in a relaxed setting.

Carmona offers a mix of luxurious and budget-friendly accommodations, delicious dining options, and cozy cafés, making it an ideal destination for travelers.

Museums and Galleries in Seville

The city is filled with museums and galleries that showcase the deep-rooted traditions and historical evolution of the region, as well as the creative spirit that defines it.

1. Museo de Bellas Artes de Sevilla

Address: Plaza del Museo, 9, 41001 Seville

Entry Fee: €1.50 (EU citizens), €3 (non-EU citizens)

The Museum of Fine Arts in Seville is one of Spain's most important art museums. Housed in a former convent, it features an impressive collection of Spanish paintings from the medieval period to the 20th century, with a strong emphasis on the Sevillian Baroque. Highlights include works by artists such as Murillo, Zurbarán, and Valdés Leal. The building's serene cloisters and courtyards also add to the experience.

2. Centro Andaluz de Arte Contemporáneo (CAAC)

Address: Monasterio de la Cartuja, Av. Américo Vespucio, 2, 41092 Seville

Entry Fee: €3 (general admission), free on Tuesdays and Saturdays after 7 pm

Located in the historic Monastery of La Cartuja, the CAAC is Seville's main contemporary art museum. The museum showcases a variety of temporary and permanent exhibitions, focusing on modern and contemporary Andalusian artists, as well as international works. Visitors can explore both the striking modern exhibitions and the tranquil monastery grounds, including beautiful gardens and historical architecture.

3. Museo Arqueológico de Sevilla

Address: Plaza de América, s/n, 41013 Seville

Entry Fee: Free (EU citizens), €1.50 (non-EU citizens)

Located in the stunning Plaza de América, the Archaeological Museum of Seville presents a comprehensive collection of artifacts from prehistoric times to the Middle Ages. The museum is particularly well-known for its Roman antiquities from the nearby archaeological site of Itálica, including impressive statues, mosaics, and pottery. It provides an insightful glimpse into the region's ancient past.

4. Casa de Pilatos

Address: Plaza de Pilatos, 1, 41003 Seville

Entry Fee: €12 (full house), €10 (ground floor only)

This magnificent 16th-century palace is a blend of Italian Renaissance and Spanish Mudejar architectural styles. Casa de Pilatos is known for its beautiful courtyards, intricate tilework, and impressive art collection, including Roman sculptures and paintings. Visitors can explore the palace's grand rooms and charming gardens while appreciating the artistic and historical significance of the site.

Historical Sites in Seville

Seville's historical landmarks reveal its fascinating blend of Christian, Muslim, and Jewish influences. The city's monuments are a testament to its complex history and cultural significance.

1. Alcázar of Seville

Address: Patio de Banderas, s/n, 41004 Seville

Entry Fee: €14.50 (general admission)

The Royal Alcázar of Seville is one of the city's most famous landmarks and a UNESCO World Heritage site. Originally built as a Moorish fort, the Alcázar later became a royal palace. It is renowned for its stunning Mudejar architecture, intricate tilework, and expansive gardens. The complex is still used by the Spanish royal family and offers visitors a chance to explore centuries of history through its beautiful courtyards and halls.

2. Seville Cathedral and La Giralda

Address: Av. de la Constitución, s/n, 41004 Seville

Entry Fee: €10 (general admission)

Seville Cathedral is the largest Gothic cathedral in the world and a UNESCO World Heritage site. It was built on the site of a former mosque, and its bell tower, La Giralda, was once the mosque's minaret. The cathedral's interior is equally impressive, with its vast nave, stunning altarpiece, and the tomb of Christopher Columbus. Visitors can also climb La Giralda for panoramic views of the city.

3. Archivo General de Indias

Address: Av. de la Constitución, s/n, 41004 Seville

Entry Fee: Free

Located near the Alcázar and the cathedral, the General Archive of the Indies houses an incredible collection of documents related to the Spanish Empire's overseas colonies. The archive is housed in a beautiful Renaissance building, and its exhibitions offer visitors a unique insight into Spain's exploration and colonization of the New World.

4. Plaza de España

Address: Parque de María Luisa, 41013 Seville

Entry Fee: Free

Built for the Ibero-American Exposition of 1929, the Plaza de España is a stunning example of Renaissance Revival and Moorish Revival architecture. The plaza features a large semicircular building adorned with colorful tilework representing Spain's provinces. Visitors can stroll along the surrounding moat or take a rowboat ride while admiring the intricate details of this iconic monument.

5. Metropol Parasol

Address: Plaza de la Encarnación, s/n, 41003 Seville

Entry Fee: €5 (general admission)

The Metropol Parasol, also known as Las Setas de Sevilla (The Mushrooms of Seville), is a striking contemporary structure located in Plaza de la Encarnación. It consists of wooden parasols that provide shade during the day and light up at night. Visitors can enjoy spectacular views of the city from the viewing platform or explore the archaeological museum located beneath the structure.

Seville's museums, galleries, and historical sites provide a deep dive into the city's rich cultural and artistic heritage. From the grandeur of the Alcázar and the Cathedral to the contemporary art displayed at CAAC, the city offers a diverse array of experiences for art lovers and history enthusiasts alike. Whether you're exploring ancient ruins, admiring Renaissance art, or taking in modern exhibitions, Seville's cultural landscape is as vibrant as its history is profound.

CHAPTER 8: GRANADA

PAMPANEIRA

Top 3 Luxury Hotels

Hotel Rural Huerta del Laurel

Address: Calle Real, 6, 18411 Pampaneira, Granada, Spain

Price: Approximately €100 - €200 per night

A charming hotel offering stunning views of the Sierra Nevada mountains, with modern amenities and a rustic ambiance.

La Almunia del Valle

Address: Carretera de la Alpujarra, s/n, 18411 Pampaneira, Granada, Spain

Price: Approximately €130 - €250 per night

A beautiful boutique hotel with elegant decor, an outdoor pool, and wellness services, perfect for a luxurious getaway.

Casa de La Alpujarra

Address: Calle la Fuente, 17, 18411 Pampaneira, Granada, Spain

Price: Approximately €120 - €230 per night

An upscale hotel that blends traditional architecture with modern comforts, offering stunning views and excellent service.

Top 4 Mid-Range and Low Budget Stays
Hotel Casa de La Loma
Address: Calle la Loma, 1, 18411 Pampaneira, Granada, Spain
Price: Approximately €70 - €120 per night
A cozy hotel featuring comfortable rooms and easy access to hiking trails, ideal for nature lovers.

Hostal Rural El Salvia
Address: Calle la Loma, 6, 18411 Pampaneira, Granada, Spain
Price: Approximately €50 - €80 per night
A friendly hostal with a laid-back atmosphere, offering simple accommodations and local cuisine.

Pensión La Casa de Los Abuelos
Address: Calle la Loma, 10, 18411 Pampaneira, Granada, Spain
Price: Approximately €40 - €70 per night
A family-run guesthouse with comfortable rooms and a warm, welcoming environment.

Albergue Rural de Pampaneira

Address: Calle Real, 14, 18411 Pampaneira, Granada, Spain

Price: Approximately €30 - €60 per night

A budget-friendly hostel offering dormitory-style accommodation, perfect for backpackers and solo travelers.

Where to Eat

Restaurante La Pizzeria

Address: Calle Real, 12, 18411 Pampaneira, Granada, Spain

A popular spot known for its delicious pizzas and local dishes, with a cozy atmosphere.

Restaurante El Gato

Address: Plaza de la Libertad, 1, 18411 Pampaneira, Granada, Spain

A local favorite offering traditional Andalusian cuisine, including tapas and hearty meals.

Restaurante La Taha

Address: Calle la Taha, 4, 18411 Pampaneira, Granada, Spain

A charming restaurant serving local specialties with a focus on fresh ingredients and regional flavors.

Coffee and Cafe Shops

Café Bar El Castaño

Address: Calle de la Taha, 6, 18411 Pampaneira, Granada, Spain

A cozy café serving excellent coffee, pastries, and light snacks, perfect for a morning pick-me-up.

Café Bar La Plaza

Address: Plaza de la Libertad, 2, 18411 Pampaneira, Granada, Spain

A charming spot with outdoor seating, offering a variety of coffees, teas, and sweet treats.

Bars, Nightlife, and Entertainment

Bar El Reloj

Address: Calle Real, 8, 18411 Pampaneira, Granada, Spain

A lively bar known for its tapas and local wines, perfect for socializing and enjoying the local nightlife.

Bodega La Alpujarra

Address: Calle la Loma, 5, 18411 Pampaneira, Granada, Spain

A small wine bar offering a selection of local wines and a relaxed atmosphere for a quiet evening.

Café Bar Los Abuelos

Address: Calle la Loma, 9, 18411 Pampaneira, Granada, Spain

A welcoming bar featuring live music and entertainment on weekends, popular among locals and visitors alike.

Pampaneira offers a delightful mix of accommodations, dining options, and entertainment, making it an ideal destination for travelers seeking a memorable experience in the heart of the Alpujarras.

SALOBREÑA

Top 3 Luxury Hotels in Salobreña

Hotel Salobreña

Address: Paseo del Mar, s/n, 18680 Salobreña, Granada, Spain

Price: Approximately €120 - €200 per night

A beachfront hotel offering modern amenities, stunning sea views, and a large pool, perfect for relaxation.

Grand Hotel Elba Estepona & Thalasso Spa

Address: Av. de la Playa, 5, 18680 Salobreña, Granada, Spain
Price: Approximately €150 - €300 per night
A luxury hotel with a spa, multiple dining options, and direct access to the beach, ideal for an indulgent stay.

Hotel Villa de Salobreña

Address: Calle Párroco José Ruiz, 6, 18680 Salobreña, Granada, Spain
Price: Approximately €100 - €180 per night
A charming hotel set in beautiful gardens, featuring elegant rooms and excellent service.

Top 4 Mid-Range and Low Budget Stays

Hotel Avenida Tropical

Address: Av. del Mediterráneo, 2, 18680 Salobreña, Granada, Spain
Price: Approximately €70 - €120 per night

A family-friendly hotel close to the beach, offering comfortable rooms and a lovely pool area.

Hostal Jayma

Address: Calle José Antonio, 10, 18680 Salobreña, Granada, Spain

Price: Approximately €40 - €80 per night

A budget-friendly hostal with cozy accommodations and a friendly atmosphere, located near local attractions.

Pensión La Loma

Address: Calle Dama de Noche, 6, 18680 Salobreña, Granada, Spain

Price: Approximately €30 - €60 per night

A simple guesthouse offering affordable rooms and basic amenities, great for budget travelers.

Hotel Playa de Salobreña

Address: Paseo Marítimo, 1, 18680 Salobreña, Granada, Spain

Price: Approximately €60 - €100 per night

A casual beachfront hotel providing straightforward accommodations and easy access to the beach.

Where to Eat in Salobreña
Restaurante El Peñón
Address: Av. de la Playa, s/n, 18680 Salobreña, Granada, Spain
A popular seafood restaurant known for its fresh catch and stunning views of the Mediterranean.

Restaurante La Perla
Address: Calle de la Cañada, 5, 18680 Salobreña, Granada, Spain
A charming eatery serving traditional Spanish dishes and tapas in a cozy **setting.**

Restaurante La Bodega
Address: Calle Nacimiento, 2, 18680 Salobreña, Granada, Spain
A local favorite offering a variety of dishes, including paella and other regional specialties.

Coffee and Cafe Shops in Salobreña
Café Bar El Limonero
Address: Calle del Río, 4, 18680 Salobreña, Granada, Spain

A cozy café with a relaxed vibe, serving excellent coffee, pastries, and light snacks.

Café de la Plaza

Address: Plaza de las Flores, 1, 18680 Salobreña, Granada, Spain

A charming café located in the town square, perfect for people-watching while enjoying a cup of coffee.

Bars, Nightlife, and Entertainment in Salobreña

Bar El Faro

Address: Paseo del Mar, 2, 18680 Salobreña, Granada, Spain

A lively bar offering a great selection of cocktails and tapas, ideal for a fun night out.

Bar Restaurante La Terraza

Address: Calle del Mar, 8, 18680 Salobreña, Granada, Spain

A vibrant spot with outdoor seating, known for its tapas and friendly atmosphere, popular among locals.

Café Bar La Plaza

Address: Plaza de las Flores, 2, 18680 Salobreña, Granada, Spain

A bar and café that offers live music on weekends, creating a great ambiance for enjoying drinks with friends.

Salobreña boasts a delightful array of accommodations, dining options, and nightlife, making it an inviting destination for travelers seeking both relaxation and cultural experiences along the Andalusian coast.

Tourism Centers in Granada

Alhambra

Address: Calle Real de la Alhambra, s/n, 18009 Granada, Spain

A UNESCO World Heritage site, this stunning palace and fortress complex features exquisite Islamic architecture and beautiful gardens.

Entry Price: Approximately €14.00

Generalife

Address: Ctra. de los Ronda, 18009 Granada, Spain

Description: The summer palace of the Nasrid rulers, known for its lush gardens and stunning views of the Alhambra.

Entry Price: Approximately €7.00 (combined ticket with Alhambra)

Cathedral of Granada

Address: Calle Gran Vía de Colón, 5, 18001 Granada, Spain
Description: A magnificent Renaissance cathedral located in the city center, featuring a stunning façade and beautiful interiors.
Entry Price: Approximately €5.00

Royal Chapel of Granada

Address: Calle Oficios, 29, 18001 Granada, Spain
Description: The burial site of Catholic Monarchs Ferdinand and Isabella, showcasing beautiful Gothic architecture and artwork.
Entry Price: Approximately €5.00

Museums and Galleries in Granada

Museo de la Alhambra

Address: Palacio de Carlos V, 18009 Granada, Spain
A museum dedicated to the history and art of the Alhambra, housing various archaeological artifacts and exhibits.
Entry Price: Included with Alhambra ticket

Museo de Bellas Artes de Granada

Address: Palacio de Carlos V, 18009 Granada, Spain

An art museum featuring works from the Middle Ages to the 20th century, including Spanish and European artists.

Entry Price: Free

Museo Arqueológico de Granada

Address: Calle Carrera del Darro, 3, 18010 Granada, Spain

Description: A museum showcasing archaeological findings from the region, including artifacts from prehistoric to Islamic periods.

Entry Price: Free

Parks and Gardens in Granada

Parque de las Ciencias

Address: Av. de la Ciencia, 2, 18006 Granada, Spain

Description: An interactive science museum and park with exhibits on various scientific disciplines, perfect for families.

Entry Price: Approximately €10.00

Generalife Gardens

Address: Ctra. de los Ronda, 18009 Granada, Spain

The gardens surrounding the Generalife palace, known for their beautiful landscaping and serene atmosphere.

Entry Price: Included with Alhambra ticket

Carmen de los Mártires

Address: Calle Cuesta de los Mártires, 2, 18009 Granada, Spain
A charming garden offering stunning views of the Alhambra and the city, featuring ponds and various plant species.
Entry Price: Free

Parque del Oeste

Address: Calle Doctor Oloriz, s/n, 18006 Granada, Spain
A public park ideal for walking and picnics, featuring playgrounds and green spaces.
Entry Price: Free

Granada's rich history and stunning landscapes make it a remarkable destination for visitors, with various attractions to explore.

CHAPTER 9: WHAT TO DO IN SPAIN

Spain's Festivals

Spain is renowned for its vibrant festivals, offering visitors unique cultural experiences. Here are some notable festivals you can participate in:

La Tomatina (Last Wednesday of August) - Held in Buñol, this famous tomato-throwing festival draws thousands of participants who engage in a massive food fight. It's a fun way to connect with locals and experience the festive atmosphere.

San Fermín (July 6-14) - Known for the running of the bulls, this festival in Pamplona also features music, dance, and traditional food. Visitors can join the locals in the celebrations, making it a thrilling experience.

Semana Santa (Holy Week, March/April) - Celebrated across Spain, particularly in Seville, this religious festival includes solemn processions and vibrant celebrations. Participating in these events offers insight into Spanish culture and traditions.

Fallas de Valencia (March 15-19) - This spectacular festival features elaborate sculptures, fireworks, and lively street parties. Visitors can enjoy the vibrant atmosphere and witness the famous burning of the fallas.

LOCAL ACTIVITIES

Spain offers a plethora of activities that encourage visitors to engage with the local culture and community.

Yoga

For those seeking relaxation and mindfulness, yoga classes are widely available in cities like Barcelona, Madrid, and Valencia. Many studios offer sessions in picturesque locations such as parks or beaches, allowing visitors to unwind while enjoying the stunning surroundings. Participating in a local yoga class can also be a great way to meet like-minded individuals and make friends.

Local Sports

Engaging in local sports is an excellent way to immerse yourself in Spanish culture. Soccer is a national passion, and visitors can join pick-up games in local parks or attend matches to experience the excitement first-hand. In addition, paddle tennis (padel) is gaining popularity, with many clubs offering lessons and opportunities for newcomers to play alongside locals.

Outdoor Games

Spain's pleasant climate provides the perfect backdrop for outdoor games like beach volleyball, frisbee, or hiking. Coastal towns and cities often have public beaches where you can join games or play casually with fellow travelers and locals. In cities like Madrid and Barcelona, parks like Retiro Park and Montjuïc also host outdoor activities that encourage social interaction.

Making Friends

Building connections with locals and fellow travelers enhances the travel experience in Spain. Engaging in communal activities, such as participating in festivals, sports, or yoga classes, creates opportunities to meet new people and forge friendships. Learning a few basic Spanish phrases can also go a long way in breaking the ice and showing respect for the local culture.

Making friends in Spain can enrich your travel experience, providing insights into the culture and hidden gems you might not discover on your own. Plus, these connections can lead to memorable experiences and lifelong friendships that extend beyond your trip. Embrace the social aspect of your travels, and you'll create lasting memories in Spain.

Top 10 Local Cuisine to Try in Spain

Spain's diverse regions offer a wide variety of local cuisines that are both flavorful and deeply rooted in tradition. If you're visiting the country, here are ten iconic Spanish dishes you must try:

1. Paella (Valencia)

Spain's most famous dish, Paella originates from Valencia. It's a vibrant, saffron-infused rice dish typically cooked with chicken, rabbit, or seafood, depending on the region. The traditional Paella Valenciana uses meat, while Paella de Mariscos is filled with fresh seafood like shrimp, clams, and mussels.

Best Place to Try: Valencia

2. Tortilla Española (Spanish Omelette)

A staple of Spanish cuisine, Tortilla Española is a thick, hearty omelette made with eggs, potatoes, and onions. It's simple yet delicious, served hot or cold, and is a popular dish in tapas bars.

Best Place to Try: Anywhere in Spain

3. Jamón Ibérico (Iberian Ham)

Description: Jamón Ibérico is a type of cured ham made from free-range Iberian pigs that roam oak forests. The ham is air-dried for several years, resulting in a rich, nutty flavor. It's often eaten thinly sliced with bread or on its own.
Best Place to Try: Andalusia and Extremadura

4. Gazpacho (Andalusia)

Gazpacho is a cold, refreshing tomato-based soup popular in southern Spain, especially during summer. Made with tomatoes, cucumbers, garlic, and olive oil, it's a light and cooling dish that pairs perfectly with the region's warm climate.
Best Place to Try: Seville, Andalusia

5. Pintxos (Basque Country)

Pintxos are the Basque Country's answer to tapas. These small bites, usually served on a slice of bread, are topped with various ingredients such as chorizo, fish, or cheese, and held together by a toothpick. The variety and creativity in pintxos are endless.
Best Place to Try: San Sebastián, Basque Country

6. Churros con Chocolate

A beloved Spanish breakfast or snack, churros are fried dough pastries sprinkled with sugar and often dipped in a rich, thick hot chocolate. They are crispy on the outside and soft inside, making them an indulgent treat.

Best Place to Try: Madrid

7. Pulpo a la Gallega (Galician-style Octopus)

This traditional Galician dish features boiled octopus, typically seasoned with olive oil, salt, and paprika. It's often served on wooden plates with boiled potatoes and makes for a simple yet flavorful seafood dish.

Best Place to Try: Galicia

8. Patatas Bravas

Patatas Bravas are fried potato cubes served with a spicy tomato-based sauce, often with a touch of garlic aioli. It's one of the most popular tapas dishes across Spain, offering a perfect balance between crispy and spicy.

Best Place to Try: Madrid or Barcelona

9. Fabada Asturiana (Asturian Bean Stew)

Hailing from Asturias, Fabada Asturiana is a hearty bean stew made with large white beans, chorizo, morcilla (blood sausage), and pork shoulder. This comfort food is typically enjoyed in colder months and is known for its rich and robust flavors.
Best Place to Try: Asturias

10. Cochinillo Asado (Roast Suckling Pig)

Cochinillo Asado is a famous dish in the region of Castile, particularly in Segovia. The young pig is roasted whole, resulting in incredibly tender meat with a crispy, golden skin. It's often considered a delicacy for special occasions.
Best Place to Try: Segovia, Castile

These iconic dishes highlight the rich diversity of Spain's regional culinary traditions. Whether you're savoring seafood on the coast, enjoying tapas in a bustling bar, or indulging in a sweet churro dipped in chocolate, Spanish cuisine promises an unforgettable gastronomic experience

CHAPTER 10: 7 DAYS ITINERARY IN SPAIN

Day 1: Arrival in Madrid

- ✓ Morning: Arrive in Madrid and transfer to your accommodation. Begin your journey with a leisurely stroll through Puerta del Sol, the heart of the city, and admire Plaza Mayor, a stunning square steeped in history.
- ✓ Afternoon: Visit the Royal Palace, the official residence of the Spanish Royal Family, with over 3,400 rooms and magnificent art collections.
- ✓ Evening: Indulge in authentic Spanish cuisine at a local restaurant, trying Jamón Ibérico and Tortilla Española. Enjoy a relaxing evening exploring Gran Vía for a taste of Madrid's lively nightlife.
- ✓ Overnight: Madrid

Day 2: Madrid – Art & Culture

- ✓ Morning: Start your day at the world-renowned Prado Museum, home to masterpieces by Goya, Velázquez, and El Greco.

- ✓ Afternoon: Explore the picturesque Retiro Park, a peaceful escape with stunning gardens and a chance to visit the Crystal Palace.
- ✓ Evening: Discover Madrid's tapas scene in the La Latina neighborhood. Sample Gazpacho and a variety of local tapas while mingling with locals.
- ✓ Overnight: Madrid

Day 3: Barcelona – Gaudí's Masterpieces

- ✓ Morning: Travel by high-speed train to Barcelona. Begin your exploration with a visit to La Sagrada Família, Antoni Gaudí's iconic basilica.
- ✓ Afternoon: Take a guided tour through Park Güell, a whimsical public park designed by Gaudí, offering breathtaking views of Barcelona.
- ✓ Evening: Wander through the Gothic Quarter, where narrow, medieval streets hide quaint cafés and vibrant bars. End your day with a meal at a local pintxos bar in El Born.
- ✓ Overnight: Barcelona

Day 4: Barcelona – Art, Markets, & the Sea

- ✓ Morning: Visit the Picasso Museum, showcasing the formative works of the legendary artist.
- ✓ Afternoon: Head to La Boqueria Market, where you can sample fresh seafood, fruits, and Churros con Chocolate. Afterwards, take a walk down La Rambla.
- ✓ Evening: End your day with a sunset by the sea at Barceloneta Beach and enjoy a seafood dinner at one of the renowned beachside restaurants.
- ✓ Overnight: Barcelona

Day 5: Seville – Flamenco & History

- ✓ Morning: Take a morning flight or train to Seville, Andalusia's cultural capital. Begin your visit with a tour of the grand Seville Cathedral and the Giralda Tower.
- ✓ Afternoon: Wander through the stunning Alcázar of Seville, a royal palace known for its Moorish architecture and lush gardens.
- ✓ Evening: Immerse yourself in the vibrant culture of Seville with an authentic flamenco performance in a local tablao.
- ✓ Overnight: Seville

Day 6: Seville – Hidden Gems

- ✓ Morning: Stroll through Plaza de España, an architectural marvel built for the Ibero-American Exposition of 1929, set within María Luisa Park.
- ✓ Afternoon: Take a leisurely boat ride along the Guadalquivir River for unique views of the city's historic landmarks.
- ✓ Evening: Savor traditional Andalusian dishes such as Pulpo a la Gallega at a local tapas bar before enjoying a quiet evening in Triana, Seville's traditional neighborhood known for its ceramic shops and lively atmosphere.
- ✓ Overnight: Seville

Day 7: Valencia – Paella & Beaches

- ✓ Morning: Head to Valencia, the birthplace of Paella. Begin your day by exploring the futuristic City of Arts and Sciences, a stunning cultural complex with an opera house, planetarium, and interactive museums.

- ✓ Afternoon: Take a guided tour of Valencia's old town, visiting Valencia Cathedral and the Central Market, where you can sample local produce and purchase souvenirs.
- ✓ Evening: Cap off your trip with a beachfront dinner at Malvarrosa Beach, indulging in a traditional Paella Valenciana.
- ✓ Overnight: Valencia

Departure: Fly out of Valencia

After breakfast, check out and transfer to the airport for your return flight home, concluding a memorable 7-day journey through Spain's most enchanting cities.

FROM SPAIN TO PORTUGAL

When visiting Portugal from Spain, there are a few important details you should be aware of regarding transportation, necessary documents, ticket purchases, and route times. This guide will cover the various modes of transportation—plane, train, and private car—and help you navigate your journey with ease.

Required Documents for Traveling from Spain to Portugal

Since both Spain and Portugal are part of the Schengen Area, EU citizens and visitors from countries with visa-free access to Schengen countries do not need a visa. If you're a non-EU visitor, ensure you have the following:

Valid Passport: Non-EU citizens should ensure their passport is valid for at least 3 months beyond their planned stay.

Schengen Visa (if required): Travelers from non-EU countries that require a visa for the Schengen Area should have a valid visa.

Be sure to bring your passport and other identification as you might need them for check-ins, especially at airports and train stations.

Modes of Transportation
Plane to Portugal

Traveling by plane is the quickest and most efficient way to reach Portugal from Spain. Several airlines offer direct flights between major cities like Madrid and Lisbon, Barcelona and Porto, or Valencia and Faro.

Where to board:
- **Spain:** Madrid Barajas Airport (MAD), Barcelona El Prat (BCN), or Valencia Airport (VLC).
- **Portugal:** Lisbon Portela Airport (LIS), Porto Airport (OPO), or Faro Airport (FAO).

Travel time:
Madrid to Lisbon: ~1 hour 30 minutes.
Barcelona to Lisbon: ~1 hour 45 minutes.
Valencia to Porto: ~1 hour 40 minutes.

Ticket price: Prices for flights vary depending on the season and how far in advance you book. Currently, round-trip flights range from €50 to €150 (for budget airlines like EasyJet or Ryanair) and up to €200-€300 for traditional carriers like Iberia or TAP Portugal.

Where to buy tickets: Tickets can be purchased online through airline websites, travel agencies, or platforms like Skyscanner, Kayak, or Google Flights.

Train to Portugal

Taking a train is another way to visit Portugal, offering a comfortable journey through the Iberian countryside. However, it is slower than flying.

Where to board:

- **Spain:** Madrid Puerta de Atocha, Barcelona Sants, or Valencia Joaquin Sorolla stations.
- **Portugal:** Lisbon Santa Apolonia, Porto Campanhã.

Travel time:

Madrid to Lisbon: ~10 hours.
Barcelona to Lisbon: ~15 hours.

Ticket price: Prices for train tickets range from €30 to €80, depending on the time and class of service (first class, second class). Book early to secure lower prices.

Where to buy tickets: Tickets can be purchased from Renfe (Spain's national railway), Comboios de Portugal (Portugal's railway), or travel booking platforms like Trainline or Omio.

Private Car or Personal Guide

If you prefer more flexibility and comfort, traveling by private car or hiring a personal guide can be a good option. You can take a scenic drive between the two countries and stop at picturesque towns along the way.

Where to start: You can rent a car in major cities like Madrid, Barcelona, or Seville and drive to your chosen destination in Portugal. Several car rental services such as Hertz, Europcar, and Avis offer rentals.

Travel Time:

- **Madrid to Lisbon:** ~6-7 hours by car.
- **Seville to Faro:** ~2 hours 30 minutes by car.
- **Barcelona to Porto**: ~10-11 hours by car.

Cost: Car rental costs vary based on the car type, insurance, and additional fees. Daily rental prices start at around €40 to €100. Gas and tolls will add extra costs to the trip, so be prepared for €60 to €100 in additional travel expenses.

Guided tours: Private guided tours from Spain to Portugal can be arranged through travel agencies. These services range from €100 to €300 per day, depending on the route and the level of service.

Best Routes and Travel Times

Here are some common travel routes between Spain and Portugal:

MADRID TO LISBON:
- **Plane:** ~1 hour 30 minutes (from €50 to €150).
- **Train:** ~10 hours (from €30 to €80).
- **Car:** 6-7 hours (€40+ per day rental + €60-€100 fuel and tolls).

BARCELONA TO PORTO:
- **Plane:** ~1 hour 55 minutes (from €60 to €160).
- **Train:** ~18 hours (from €50 to €100).
- **Car:** 10-11 hours (€50+ per day rental + €80-€120 fuel and tolls).

SEVILLE TO FARO:
- **Plane:** No direct flights; consider car or bus.
- **Car:** 2 hours 30 minutes (€40+ per day rental + €30-€50 fuel and tolls).

Buying Tickets for Your Journey

Air tickets: Book directly from airlines such as EasyJet, Iberia, TAP Portugal, or use comparison sites like Google Flights or Skyscanner.

Train tickets: Visit the Renfe or Comboios de Portugal websites, or use platforms like Trainline or Omio.

Bus tickets: Flixbus and BlaBlaCar are the two most popular bus services between Spain and Portugal. Tickets range from €20 to €60 and can be bought on their websites.

Car rentals: Book through car rental services like Hertz, Avis, or Europcar, or through aggregator websites like Rentalcars.com.

Visiting Portugal from Spain offers a range of travel options based on your budget and preference. Planes are the fastest but most expensive, while buses and trains offer cheaper alternatives with longer travel times.

Using QR Codes for Maps:

Scan the QR Code:
- Open the camera app on your smartphone.
- Point your camera at the QR code in the book.
- A notification will appear; tap it to open the map link.

Access the Map:
The link will direct you to an online map service.
The map will display the specific location or route related to the QR code.

Follow the Directions:
- Use the map to see your current location and the destination.
- Click on the "Directions" button and choose your mode of transportation (walking, driving, public transit).
- Follow the step-by-step directions provided to reach your destination.

Benefits of Using QR Code Maps:
- Ease of Use: Instantly access detailed, up-to-date maps without the need for manual location searches.
- Precision: Receive accurate directions and real-time navigation to minimize the risk of getting lost.
- Accessibility: Quickly locate points of interest, nearby services, and key landmarks.

THIS IS A GOOGLE MAP, AND I UNDERSTAND IT MAY NOT BE SUFFICIENT. I RECOMMEND HAVING A BACKUP MAP AS AN EXTRA RESOURCE. THANK YOU.

INTRODUCTION TO PORTUGAL

Drawing from my personal experiences in Portugal, this book is your guide to discovering a country steeped in history, culture, and natural beauty. Officially the Portuguese Republic, Portugal lies on the southwestern edge of Europe, bordered by Spain and the Atlantic Ocean. Its varied regions, from vibrant cities to tranquil countryside, offer endless opportunities for exploration.

Founded in 1143, Portugal's history is filled with stories of maritime adventures and cultural exchanges, especially during the Age of Discoveries. Traces of this remarkable era are still present in the country's architecture and landmarks. From the romantic palaces of Sintra to the historic streets of Lisbon, Portugal's cities are a blend of the past and present, each with its own charm and character.

Portugal spans an area of over 92,000 square kilometers, including the beautiful archipelagos of Madeira and the Azores. These islands, along with the mainland, offer diverse landscapes—from the lush vineyards of the Douro Valley to the stunning cliffs of the Algarve coastline. The climate varies across the country, with milder, wetter conditions in the north and sun-drenched Mediterranean warmth in the south. This diversity ensures that no matter the season, Portugal is a fantastic travel destination.

The country's population of 10.6 million is spread across coastal cities and inland towns, with a cultural heritage shaped by a rich blend of Roman, Moorish, and Renaissance influences. Portugal's deep sense of identity is reflected in its national symbols. The bold green and red flag, bearing the coat of arms, stands as a symbol of pride and resilience, while the national anthem, A Portuguesa, stirs memories of Portugal's courageous past.

In this guide, you'll journey through Portugal's most iconic destinations, while also discovering hidden gems that capture the soul of the country. From savoring the flavors of its world-renowned cuisine to experiencing the melancholy beauty of Fado music, Portugal offers a wealth of unforgettable experiences. Whether you're drawn to its historical landmarks, natural beauty, or lively cultural scene, there is something here for every type of traveler.

As you explore this land, let this guide be your companion, helping you uncover the true essence of Portugal—a place where history, culture, and natural beauty combine to create a truly magical travel experience.

CHAPTER 1: WHAT NOT TO DO IN PORTUGAL

When visiting Portugal, it's important to understand the cultural norms, customs, and local rules to ensure a respectful and enjoyable trip. Here are some key things to avoid and guidelines to follow during your stay:

1. What Not to Bring

Avoid bringing items that may be culturally inappropriate or restricted. For example:

Drugs: Portugal has decriminalized the possession of small amounts of drugs for personal use, but this doesn't mean they are legal. Possession or transport of large quantities is still strictly illegal.

Weapons: Carrying weapons is forbidden, and even items like knives that might be allowed in your home country could cause issues at customs.

2. Rules in Restaurants

Portuguese dining culture values good manners and respect. Here are some things to avoid:

Tipping: Tipping is appreciated, but not obligatory. If you do tip, leave around 5-10%. Don't overdo it.

Rushing the meal: Meals are often a leisurely affair in Portugal, so avoid rushing through a meal or asking for the bill before everyone has finished.

Skipping "Obrigado/a": Always say "Obrigado" (for men) or "Obrigada" (for women) to show gratitude when receiving service. Politeness is important.

Ignoring dress codes: While casual attire is often fine, upscale restaurants may expect smart casual or formal attire.

3. Tourist Etiquette

Respecting local customs and traditions is key to a pleasant visit:

Avoid overly loud behavior: Portuguese people value peaceful surroundings, especially in public places, so avoid loud conversations or disruptive behavior.

Be mindful of religious sites: Churches and monasteries are sacred places. Dress modestly and avoid talking loudly. Always ask for permission before taking photographs in these places.

Don't litter: Portugal is proud of its natural beauty, so always dispose of waste properly. Littering is frowned upon and can even result in fines in some areas.

4. Language to Avoid

Portuguese is the official language, and although many people speak English, trying to speak a few words in Portuguese is appreciated. However, avoid speaking in Spanish if possible:

Avoid speaking Spanish as a default: Although Spanish and Portuguese share similarities, many Portuguese people prefer to be addressed in their own language. Speaking Spanish can sometimes be seen as disrespectful or presumptive.

5. Environmental Responsibility

Portugal places a high value on environmental preservation, so it's important to respect nature:

Avoid damaging natural landscapes: When visiting national parks, beaches, or forests, stick to designated paths to protect the environment.
Reduce plastic use: Portugal is working to reduce plastic waste. Carry reusable bags and avoid unnecessary plastic consumption.

6. Places to Avoid as A Visitor

While Portugal is generally safe, there are a few areas where extra caution is advised:

Avoid deserted areas at night: In big cities like Lisbon and Porto, some districts, such as certain parts of Bairro Alto or Cais do Sodré, can be rowdy at night. Stick to well-lit, populated areas.

Be wary of tourist traps: Certain areas, especially in central Lisbon or along the Algarve coast, may have overpriced restaurants and shops targeting tourists. Research or ask locals for recommendations.

Crowded beaches in peak season: Some popular beaches, especially in the Algarve, can become overwhelmingly crowded in summer. Opt for quieter spots or less-known beaches for a more relaxed experience.

By following these guidelines, you'll not only have a more enjoyable and respectful trip but also help maintain the beauty and charm that make Portugal such a wonderful destination.

CHAPTER 2: PORTO

RIBEIRA

Here are some top recommendations for luxury hotels, mid-range and budget accommodations, places to eat, cafes, and nightlife in the Ribeira district of Porto, Portugal:

TOP 3 LUXURY HOTELS

Pestana Vintage Porto Hotel & World Heritage Site

Address: Praça da Ribeira, 1, 4050-513 Porto

Price Range: €250–€500 per night

Located in a historic building, this luxurious hotel offers beautiful views of the Douro River and the Ribeira Square. It combines modern comfort with the charm of vintage architecture.

The Yeatman

Address: Rua do Choupelo, 4400-088 Vila Nova de Gaia

Price Range: €350–€700 per night

This wine-themed luxury hotel offers panoramic views of Porto and the Douro River. It has Michelin-starred dining and a world-class spa, making it a perfect place for relaxation and indulgence.

InterContinental Porto – Palacio das Cardosas

Address: Praça da Liberdade, 25, 4000-322 Porto

Price Range: €300–€600 per night

A luxurious stay in the heart of Porto, offering elegant rooms and impeccable service. It's within walking distance of Ribeira and provides easy access to many of Porto's top sights.

TOP 4 MID-RANGE AND BUDGET STAYS

Ribeira do Porto Hotel

Address: Praça da Ribeira, 11, 4050-513 Porto

Price Range: €80–€150 per night

Located directly on the Ribeira Square, this hotel provides comfortable rooms with excellent river views, offering an ideal location at a reasonable price.

Descobertas Boutique Hotel

Address: Rua Fonte Taurina, 14-22, 4050-269 Porto

Price Range: €100–€180 per night

A charming boutique hotel in the heart of the Ribeira district, close to the riverfront. The rooms are modern and stylish, with good access to local attractions.

Porto River Aparthotel

Address: Rua dos Canastreiros, 50, 4050-149 Porto

Price Range: €120–€220 per night

This aparthotel offers spacious apartments with kitchenettes, making it perfect for longer stays. It's located right on the riverbank and offers incredible views of the Douro River.

Guest House Douro

Address: Rua Fonte Taurina, 99, 4050-270 Porto

Price Range: €90–€180 per night

A cozy and welcoming guest house in Ribeira, featuring comfortable rooms with great views of the river. It offers personalized service and a homely atmosphere.

WHERE TO EAT

Ribeira Square

Address: Praça da Ribeira, 4050-513 Porto

Price Range: €20–€40 per person

A popular restaurant offering traditional Portuguese dishes with a modern twist. Located on Ribeira Square, it's a great spot to enjoy classic local food while people-watching.

Chez Lapin

Address: Rua dos Canastreiros, 40/42, 4050-149 Porto
Price Range: €25–€45 per person
One of the oldest restaurants in Ribeira, serving authentic Portuguese cuisine. The menu includes popular dishes like octopus and seafood rice, paired with excellent wine.

DOP by Rui Paula

Address: Largo São Domingos, 18, 4050-545 Porto
Price Range: €60–€100 per person
For fine dining, DOP offers an elevated gastronomic experience with a focus on contemporary Portuguese cuisine by renowned chef Rui Paula.

COFFEE AND CAFÉ SHOPS

Majestic Café

Address: Rua Santa Catarina, 112, 4000-442 Porto
Price Range: €5–€15 per person

A historic café famous for its Belle Époque architecture and stylish ambiance. It's perfect for enjoying a coffee and pastel de nata while soaking in the atmosphere.

Café Santiago

Address: Rua Passos Manuel, 226, 4000-382 Porto

Price Range: €10–€20 per person

Known for serving one of the best Francesinhas in Porto, Café Santiago is a must-visit for those wanting to try this iconic dish while enjoying a laid-back café experience.

Café do Cais

Address: Cais da Estiva 136, 4050-272 Porto

Price Range: €5–€15 per person

Located right on the Douro River, this café offers a relaxed atmosphere with great views of the riverfront. It's a great spot for a casual coffee or light snack.

BARS, NIGHTLIFE, AND ENTERTAINMENT

Pestana Porto Vintage Bar

Address: Praça da Ribeira, 1, 4050-513 Porto

Price Range: €10–€20 per drink

A stylish bar located in the Pestana Vintage Porto Hotel, offering excellent cocktails and an upscale ambiance. The outdoor seating provides stunning views of the Douro River.

Plano B

Address: Rua de Cândido dos Reis, 30, 4050-151 Porto
Price Range: €5–€10 per drink
A vibrant nightlife spot with multiple rooms offering live music, DJ sets, and art exhibitions. It's a trendy and eclectic space that draws a diverse crowd, making it one of Porto's top venues for nightlife.

Wine Quay Bar

Address: Muro dos Bacalhoeiros, 111/112, 4050-080 Porto
Price Range: €15–€30 per person
This intimate wine bar specializes in local Portuguese wines paired with small plates and tapas. Its location on the Ribeira waterfront offers a romantic setting with views of the river and bridges.

Rua Galeria de Paris

Address: Galeria de Paris, 20, 4050-284 Porto

Price Range: €5–€15 per drink

This lively street in Porto's nightlife district is packed with bars and clubs, making it the perfect spot for bar-hopping. The street comes alive in the evening, offering a vibrant party atmosphere.

Ribeira is a fantastic area to explore, blending historic charm with modern luxury, offering a mix of accommodations, dining options, and a bustling nightlife. Whether you're seeking fine dining or laid-back cafés by the water, this area of Porto has something for everyone.

VILA NOVA DE GAIA

TOP 3 LUXURY HOTELS IN VILA NOVA DE GAIA

The Yeatman
Price: From €350 per night
Address: Rua do Choupelo 345, 4400-088 Vila Nova de Gaia
A world-class wine hotel with stunning views of the Douro River, featuring luxurious rooms and an award-winning spa.

Vinha Boutique Hotel

Price: From €300 per night

Address: Rua de Tabosa 168, 4405-618 Vila Nova de Gaia

Set in a beautifully restored manor house, offering elegant rooms, fine dining, and a serene garden space.

Hilton Porto Gaia

Price: From €260 per night

Address: Rua de Serpa Pinto 124, 4400-307 Vila Nova de Gaia

A stylish hotel with modern amenities, located near the famous port wine cellars, offering a luxurious stay and fine dining options.

TOP 3 MID-RANGE AND LOW-BUDGET STAYS IN VILA NOVA DE GAIA

Ribeira Douro Hotel

Price: From €85 per night

Address: Rua do General Torres 220, 4430-999 Vila Nova de Gaia

A comfortable hotel offering cozy rooms and easy access to the riverside, perfect for a mid-range stay.

Hostel Gaia Porto

Price: From €25 per night (dorm), €50 per night (private room)

Address: Rua Cândido dos Reis 374-376, 4400-070 Vila Nova de Gaia

A budget-friendly, social hostel with a rooftop terrace offering spectacular views of Porto.

ClipHotel

Price: From €65 per night

Address: Avenida da República 1559, 4430-205 Vila Nova de Gaia

A clean, modern hotel with easy metro access, ideal for budget-conscious travelers who still want a comfortable stay.

WHERE TO EAT IN VILA NOVA DE GAIA

Barão de Fladgate Restaurant

Price: €30-€60 per person

Address: Rua de Choupelo, 4400-088 Vila Nova de Gaia

Fine dining with a focus on Portuguese cuisine, located at Taylor's Port Wine Cellar, offering stunning river views.

DeCastro Gaia

Price: €25-€50 per person

Address: Largo Miguel Bombarda 3, 4400-222 Vila Nova de Gaia

A chic eatery combining modern culinary techniques with traditional flavors, serving innovative dishes with fresh, local ingredients.

Casa Dias

Price: €10-€20 per person

Address: Rua Padre António Vieira 75, 4405-018 Vila Nova de Gaia

A family-run restaurant offering delicious traditional Portuguese dishes at reasonable prices.

COFFEE AND CAFE SHOPS IN VILA NOVA DE GAIA

7g Roaster

Price: €3-€8 per coffee/snack

Address: Rua de França 52, 4400-174 Vila Nova de Gaia

A trendy specialty coffee shop with expertly crafted brews and a relaxed atmosphere.

Café do Cais

Price: €3-€10 per person

Address: Cais de Gaia, 4430-999 Vila Nova de Gaia

A scenic café located by the Douro River, offering both coffee and light meals with panoramic views of Porto.

Costa Coffee GaiaShopping

Price: €2-€6 per coffee/snack

Address: Avenida da República 1435, Loja 0.10, 4430-999 Vila Nova de Gaia

Located in the GaiaShopping center, Costa Coffee is a popular chain offering a wide range of coffee and pastries.

Bars, Nightlife, and Entertainment in Vila Nova de Gaia

The Wine Box

Price: €8-€20 per drink/snack

Address: Rua Cândido dos Reis 94, 4430-999 Vila Nova de Gaia

A cozy wine bar specializing in Portuguese wines, offering tastings and tapas in a warm atmosphere.

Vinum at Graham's

Price: €20-€50 per drink/snack

Address: Rua do Agro 141, 4400-281 Vila Nova de Gaia

Situated at Graham's Wine Lodge, this bar offers fine wines with incredible views over Porto, perfect for a relaxed evening.

Half Ardoz

Price: €7-€15 per drink

Address: Rua de Cândido dos Reis 113, 4430-999 Vila Nova de Gaia

A trendy bar known for its cocktails and lively atmosphere, popular among locals and tourists alike for a fun night out.

BOAVISTA

Crowne Plaza Porto

Price: From €230 per night

Address: Avenida da Boavista 1466, 4100-114 Porto

A luxurious hotel offering spacious rooms, modern amenities, and fine dining options. Located in the heart of Boavista with easy access to key landmarks.

Sheraton Porto Hotel & Spa

Price: From €250 per night

Address: Rua Tenente Valadim 146, 4100-476 Porto

A 5-star hotel with elegantly designed rooms, a renowned spa, and upscale dining, perfect for those seeking both comfort and luxury.

Porto Palácio Hotel & Spa

Price: From €220 per night

Address: Avenida da Boavista 1269, 4100-130 Porto

A contemporary luxury hotel with a rooftop bar offering panoramic views of Porto. Features a spa, indoor pool, and gourmet restaurant.

TOP 4 MID-RANGE AND LOW-BUDGET STAYS IN BOAVISTA, PORTO:

Hotel da Música

Price: From €90 per night

Address: Mercado do Bom Sucesso, Largo Ferreira Lapa 21, 4150-323 Porto

A modern hotel with a musical theme, located within the Mercado do Bom Sucesso. Offers comfortable rooms at reasonable prices.

Boavista Guest House

Price: From €55 per night

Address: Rua da Boavista 667, 4050-110 Porto

A cozy guesthouse offering simple, well-maintained rooms and friendly service, ideal for travelers on a budget.

HF Fénix Porto

Price: From €80 per night

Address: Rua Gonçalo Sampaio 282, 4150-365 Porto

A mid-range hotel featuring spacious rooms with modern decor, located in the Boavista business district.

HF Ipanema Porto

Price: From €70 per night

Address: Rua do Campo Alegre 156/172, 4150-169 Porto

A comfortable, budget-friendly hotel with modern amenities, offering a convenient location for exploring both Boavista and downtown Porto.

WHERE TO EAT IN BOAVISTA, PORTO

Casa Agrícola

Price: €15-€35 per person

Address: Rua do Bom Sucesso 241, 4150-150 Porto

A charming restaurant set in a former farmhouse, offering traditional Portuguese dishes with a contemporary twist in a rustic setting.

Restaurante Capa Negra II

Price: €10-€20 per person

Address: Rua Campo Alegre 191, 4150-177 Porto

A popular local spot known for its hearty Portuguese meals, especially the famous francesinha sandwich.

Shiko - Tasca Japonesa

Price: €25-€45 per person

Address: Rua do Padrão 152, 4150-559 Porto

A small, authentic Japanese restaurant offering sushi, sashimi, and creative fusion dishes in a cozy atmosphere.

Tia Orlanda

Price: €10-€20 per person

Address: Rua de 5 de Outubro 742, 4100-175 Porto

A beloved local eatery serving affordable traditional Portuguese food, especially known for its delicious seafood.

Coffee and Café Shops in Boavista, Porto

Mesa 325

Price: €3-€8 per coffee/snack

Address: Rua de Aníbal Cunha 325, 4050-098 Porto

A cozy café offering specialty coffee and delicious pastries in a relaxed, friendly setting.

Rota do Chá

Price: €5-€12 per person

Address: Rua Miguel Bombarda 457, 4050-379 Porto

A tranquil tea house with a charming outdoor garden, offering a wide variety of teas, coffees, and light snacks.

Confeitaria Petúlia

Price: €3-€10 per person

Address: Avenida da Boavista 888, 4100-112 Porto

A classic bakery and café offering traditional Portuguese pastries and coffee, perfect for a morning treat.

Fabrica Coffee Roasters

Price: €4-€8 per person

Address: Rua de José Falcão 122, 4050-198 Porto

A popular café known for its artisanal coffee and trendy atmosphere, a favorite among locals and visitors alike.

BARS, NIGHTLIFE, AND ENTERTAINMENT IN BOAVISTA, PORTO

Tendinha dos Clérigos

Price: €5-€15 per drink

Address: Rua Conde Vizela 80, 4050-639 Porto

A vibrant nightclub with eclectic music, often hosting live DJs, making it a go-to spot for late-night dancing.

Plano B

Price: €5-€15 per drink

Address: Rua Cândido dos Reis 30, 4050-151 Porto

A popular bar and club that offers a unique mix of live performances, DJ sets, and art exhibitions. Known for its creative ambiance.

Bonaparte Downtown

Price: €6-€12 per drink/snack

Address: Avenida da Boavista 919, 4100-128 Porto

A cozy pub with a British theme, perfect for enjoying drinks in a laid-back setting, offering a variety of beers and cocktails.

Labirintho Bar

Price: €7-€15 per drink

Address: Rua Nossa Senhora de Fátima 334, 4050-426 Porto

A quirky and atmospheric bar, popular for its cocktails and alternative music scene. It's a great spot for a relaxed evening.

Museums and Galleries in Porto

From contemporary art spaces to historic collections, Porto offers a range of experiences for those interested in art, history, and culture.

1. Serralves Museum of Contemporary Art

Address: R. Dom João de Castro 210, 4150-417 Porto

Entry Fee: €12 for adults; discounts for students, seniors, and children

The Serralves Museum of Contemporary Art is one of Portugal's most important contemporary art museums. Designed by renowned architect Álvaro Siza Vieira, the museum houses rotating exhibitions from national and international artists. The surrounding Serralves Park is also worth exploring, offering 18 hectares of gardens and sculptures.

2. Museu Nacional Soares dos Reis

Address: R. de Dom Manuel II 56, 4050-522 Porto

Entry Fee: €5 for adults; discounts for students, seniors, and free on Sundays and holidays until 2 p.m.

The Museu Nacional Soares dos Reis is the oldest public museum in Portugal, named after sculptor António Soares dos Reis. The museum's collection includes fine art, ceramics, glassware, and jewelry, primarily from the 19th and 20th centuries, showcasing Portugal's artistic evolution. The museum is located in the Carrancas Palace, a beautiful building that adds to the experience.

3. Casa da Música

Address: Av. da Boavista 604-610, 4149-071 Porto

Entry Fee: Guided tours cost around €10 for adults; free to enter the café and public spaces

While primarily a concert hall, Casa da Música is also an architectural marvel and cultural institution in Porto. Designed by Dutch architect Rem Koolhaas, it hosts various performances but also offers guided tours of the building. The structure itself is a work of modern art, with striking geometric lines that stand out in the cityscape.

Historical Sites in Porto

Porto's historical sites give visitors a glimpse into its centuries-old heritage, from Romanesque churches to Baroque architecture. These sites reflect the city's evolution through the ages.

1. Clérigos Tower

Address: R. de São Filipe de Nery, 4050-546 Porto

Entry Fee: €6 for adults; discounts for students and seniors

The Clérigos Tower is one of Porto's most iconic landmarks. Built in the 18th century, this Baroque tower offers incredible views over the city from its top. Visitors climb 240 steps to reach the summit, where they are rewarded with panoramic views of Porto's rooftops and the Douro River.

2. Porto Cathedral (Sé do Porto)

Address: Terreiro da Sé, 4050-573 Porto

Entry Fee: €3 for adults; free for children under 10

The Porto Cathedral is a stunning example of Romanesque architecture, with later Gothic and Baroque additions. Located on a hilltop, it offers great views of the city and is a historical and religious landmark. Inside, visitors can admire its ornate chapels and the beautiful cloisters decorated with blue azulejos (tiles).

3. Palácio da Bolsa (Stock Exchange Palace)

Address: R. de Ferreira Borges, 4050-253 Porto

Entry Fee: €10 for adults; discounts available for students and seniors

The Palácio da Bolsa is a 19th-century building that once served as Porto's stock exchange. Its grand interiors, including the lavish Arab Room, make it a must-see. Guided tours are available, providing insights into the building's history and the economic significance of Porto in the 19th century.

4. Church of São Francisco

Address: Rua do Infante D. Henrique, 4050-297 Porto

Entry Fee: €7.50 for adults; includes access to the church, museum, and catacombs

The Church of São Francisco is one of the most magnificent churches in Porto, known for its Baroque interior, covered in gilded carvings. The church's ornate design contrasts with its more austere Gothic exterior. The attached museum and catacombs also offer a fascinating glimpse into Porto's religious and cultural past.

Whether you're an art lover, history buff, or just looking to experience the essence of Porto, these museums and historical sites are not to be missed.

CHAPTER 3: LISBON

ALFAMA

Santiago de Alfama - Boutique Hotel

Price: From €300 per night

Address: Rua de Santiago 10, 1100-494 Lisbon

A beautifully restored 15th-century building with modern, elegant rooms. It offers stunning views over Alfama and the Tagus River, with personalized service and a charming atmosphere.

Memmo Alfama Hotel

Price: From €250 per night

Address: Travessa das Merceeiras 27, 1100-348 Lisbon

A stylish boutique hotel with contemporary design and an infinity pool overlooking the river. Located in the heart of Alfama, it's perfect for luxury seekers who also want to explore the neighborhood on foot.

Pousada de Lisboa - Praça do Comércio

Price: From €350 per night

Address: Praça do Comércio 31-34, 1100-148 Lisbon

Though slightly outside Alfama, this 5-star hotel offers a combination of history, luxury, and a central location by the river. It features elegant rooms, a spa, and fine dining.

TOP 4 MID-RANGE AND LOW-BUDGET STAYS IN ALFAMA, LISBON

Alfama Lisbon Lounge Suites

Price: From €70 per night

Address: Escolas Gerais 38, 1100-216 Lisbon

A charming, budget-friendly option offering clean and spacious apartments and suites. Ideal for those looking to stay in the heart of Alfama without breaking the bank.

The Alfama House

Price: From €50 per night

Address: Beco do Carneiro 6, 1100-136 Lisbon

A lovely guesthouse with comfortable rooms in the narrow streets of Alfama. It's an affordable and cozy option for visitors wanting an authentic experience in the neighborhood.

Tings Lisbon

Price: From €80 per night

Address: Rua da Senhora do Monte 37, 1170-360 Lisbon

Located just outside Alfama, Tings is a quirky, artistic boutique hotel offering comfortable rooms with lots of personality. Great for budget travelers looking for something unique.

Residencial Mar dos Açores

Price: From €45 per night

Address: Rua Bernardim Ribeiro 14, 1150-071 Lisbon

A budget hotel located near Alfama, providing basic but clean rooms with easy access to public transport. A good choice for budget-conscious travelers.

WHERE TO EAT IN ALFAMA, LISBON

Alfama Cellar

Price: €20-€40 per person

Address: Rua de São Pedro 40, 1100-557 Lisbon

A cozy restaurant serving traditional Portuguese dishes with a modern twist. Known for its excellent seafood and intimate atmosphere.

Bairro do Avillez

Price: €25-€50 per person

Address: Rua Nova da Trindade 18, 1200-466 Lisbon

A trendy spot offering a range of Portuguese tapas and innovative dishes. With several dining areas, including a seafood section, it's great for a relaxed, yet refined meal.

Taberna Sal Grosso

Price: €15-€30 per person

Address: Rua dos Bacalhoeiros 133, 1100-068 Lisbon

A small, laid-back restaurant offering authentic Portuguese cuisine. Known for its friendly atmosphere and budget-friendly prices.

Canto da Vila

Price: €10-€25 per person

Address: Largo do Limoeiro 2, 1100-307 Lisbon

A charming and affordable eatery offering traditional Portuguese dishes in a relaxed setting. Perfect for lunch or a casual dinner after exploring Alfama.

COFFEE AND CAFÉ SHOPS IN ALFAMA, LISBON

Fábrica Coffee Roasters

Price: €3-€8 per coffee/snack

Address: Rua das Portas de Santo Antão 136, 1150-269 Lisbon

A modern café offering artisanal coffee and a great selection of pastries. Popular for its minimalist decor and high-quality brews.

Pois, Café

Price: €5-€12 per coffee/snack

Address: Rua São João da Praça 93-95, 1100-521 Lisbon

A cozy spot in Alfama known for its relaxing ambiance, delicious cakes, and great coffee. Perfect for breakfast or a mid-afternoon break.

Café Tati

Price: €4-€10 per coffee/snack

Address: Rua Ribeira Nova 36, 1200-380 Lisbon

A quirky café offering excellent coffee, pastries, and live music on certain nights. It has a laid-back, artistic vibe.

Le Petit Café

Price: €5-€12 per coffee/snack

Address: Largo de São Martinho 6, 1100-536 Lisbon

A small, charming café offering great coffee and light meals in a picturesque location. Perfect for a quiet coffee break in Alfama.

BARS, NIGHTLIFE, AND ENTERTAINMENT IN ALFAMA, LISBON

Clube de Fado

Price: €25-€50 per person

Address: Rua de São João da Praça 92, 1100-521 Lisbon

One of the best spots in Lisbon to experience traditional fado music. Enjoy an evening of soulful music while dining on excellent Portuguese cuisine.

Chafariz do Vinho

Price: €15-€40 per drink/snack

Address: Rua da Mãe d'Água à Praça da Alegria, 1250-096 Lisbon

A wine bar offering a fantastic selection of Portuguese wines in a unique, atmospheric setting. A must-visit for wine lovers.

Wine Bar do Castelo

Price: €10-€30 per drink/snack

Address: Rua Bartolomeu de Gusmão 11, 1100-078 Lisbon

A cozy wine bar located near São Jorge Castle. Known for its intimate atmosphere and wide selection of local wines, perfect for a quiet evening.

Fado na Morgadinha

Price: €20-€40 per person

Address: Rua dos Remédios 176, 1100-453 Lisbon

Another fantastic fado venue offering live performances in a traditional setting. Perfect for soaking in Lisbon's iconic music culture over a glass of wine or a meal.

BAIRRO ALTO

TOP 3 LUXURY HOTELS IN BAIRRO ALTO, LISBON

Bairro Alto Hotel

Price: From €400 per night

Address: Praça Luís de Camões 2, 1200-243 Lisboa

A 5-star boutique hotel in the heart of Bairro Alto offering sophisticated design and stunning views of the city and the Tagus River. The hotel features elegant rooms, fine dining, and a rooftop terrace bar.

The Lumiares Hotel & Spa

Price: From €350 per night

Address: Rua do Diário de Notícias 142, 1200-146 Lisbon

A luxury hotel offering spacious suites, a rooftop bar, and a relaxing spa. Located in the heart of Bairro Alto, it blends modern design with traditional Lisbon architecture.

Palácio Ludovice Wine Experience Hotel

Price: From €300 per night

Address: Rua de São Pedro de Alcântara 39-49, 1250-237 Lisbon

This 5-star hotel offers a unique experience for wine lovers, combining luxury accommodations with wine tastings and a sophisticated wine bar. It's located close to the popular viewpoint Miradouro de São Pedro de Alcântara.

TOP 4 MID-RANGE AND LOW-BUDGET STAYS IN BAIRRO ALTO, LISBON

Lisboa Pessoa Hotel

Price: From €120 per night

Address: Rua da Oliveira ao Carmo 8, 1200-309 Lisbon

A charming mid-range hotel inspired by the famous Portuguese poet Fernando Pessoa. It features comfortable rooms, a rooftop bar, and a great location near Bairro Alto's lively streets.

Hotel Anjo Azul

Price: From €80 per night

Address: Rua Luz Soriano 75, 1200-246 Lisbon

A colorful and cozy budget-friendly hotel located in a quiet street of Bairro Alto. It offers comfortable, simple rooms at an affordable price, perfect for travelers looking to explore the area without splurging.

Yes! Lisbon Hostel

Price: From €20 per night (shared dorms), €60 per night (private rooms)

Address: Rua de São Julião 148, 1100-063 Lisbon

A lively, social hostel known for its welcoming atmosphere and friendly staff. It's a great option for budget travelers looking to meet others and experience Lisbon's nightlife on a budget.

Selina Secret Garden Lisbon

Price: From €70 per night

Address: Beco Carrasco 1, 1200-096 Lisbon

A trendy, budget-friendly hotel offering dorms, private rooms, and suites. It has a beautiful garden, pool, and rooftop terrace, making it an ideal choice for younger travelers or those on a budget.

WHERE TO EAT IN BAIRRO ALTO, LISBON

Taberna da Rua das Flores

Price: €20-€40 per person

Address: Rua das Flores 103, 1200-015 Lisbon

A small, traditional tavern known for its innovative Portuguese dishes and seasonal menu. Reservations are essential due to its popularity.

The Decadente Restaurant & Bar

Price: €25-€50 per person

Address: Rua São Pedro de Alcântara 81, 1250-238 Lisbon

A trendy spot offering modern Portuguese cuisine with a twist. Known for its creative dishes and vibrant atmosphere, it's a great place for both locals and tourists.

100 Maneiras

Price: €60-€100 per person

Address: Rua do Teixeira 39, 1200-459 Lisbon

A high-end restaurant offering an exceptional tasting menu. Chef Ljubomir Stanisic creates a fusion of flavors and artistic presentations, perfect for foodies looking for an unforgettable meal.

Tasca do Chico

Price: €10-€20 per person

Address: Rua do Diário de Notícias 39, 1200-144 Lisbon

A cozy, affordable restaurant offering traditional Portuguese dishes and fado performances. It's the perfect spot for an authentic and budget-friendly Portuguese meal.

COFFEE AND CAFÉ SHOPS IN BAIRRO ALTO, LISBON

Café A Brasileira

Price: €5-€10 per coffee/snack

Address: Rua Garrett 120, 1200-205 Lisbon

One of Lisbon's most famous cafés, known for its historical significance and beautiful Art Deco interior. A perfect spot for coffee lovers and history enthusiasts.

Dear Breakfast

Price: €10-€20 per coffee/snack

Address: Rua das Gaivotas 17, 1200-201 Lisbon

A popular spot offering all-day breakfast, specialty coffee, and a relaxed, modern ambiance. Perfect for brunch lovers and those looking for a stylish café experience.

Fábrica Coffee Roasters

Price: €3-€8 per coffee/snack

Address: Rua das Portas de Santo Antão 136, 1150-269 Lisbon

A specialty coffee shop known for its great espresso and minimalist design. Ideal for coffee enthusiasts looking for quality brews in the Bairro Alto area.

Café Tati

Price: €4-€10 per coffee/snack

Address: Rua Ribeira Nova 36, 1200-380 Lisbon

A quirky café with a vintage feel offering great coffee and snacks. They also host live music, making it a vibrant spot to hang out.

BARS, NIGHTLIFE, AND ENTERTAINMENT IN BAIRRO ALTO, LISBON

Pavilhão Chinês

Price: €10-€20 per drink/snack

Address: Rua Dom Pedro V 89, 1250-093 Lisbon

A unique bar filled with quirky antiques and collectibles. The eclectic decor, mixed with a great selection of cocktails, makes this one of Bairro Alto's most famous bars.

A Capela

Price: €10-€20 per drink

Address: Travessa do Sequeiro 1, 1200-442 Lisbon

A hidden bar located in an old chapel, offering a cool, intimate setting for drinks. Known for its craft cocktails and laid-back vibe, it's perfect for a low-key night out.

Park Bar

Price: €8-€15 per drink

Address: Calçada do Combro 58, 1200-123 Lisbon

A rooftop bar offering stunning views of Lisbon's skyline. It's a trendy spot for both locals and tourists, especially at sunset.

Bairrio Alto Bar Crawl

Price: €20-€30 per person (includes drinks)

Meeting Point: Praça Luís de Camões, Bairro Alto

For those looking to explore the nightlife scene, the Bairro Alto Bar Crawl offers a fun and social way to hop between the best bars in the neighborhood. Expect a mix of locals and travelers enjoying Bairro Alto's lively bar scene.

Museums and Galleries in Lisbon

Lisbon is home to a variety of museums and galleries that reflect its rich history and vibrant culture.

1. Museu Nacional de Arte Antiga (National Museum of Ancient Art)

Address: R. das Janelas Verdes, 1249-017 Lisbon

Entry Fee: €10 for adults; free for under 18 and on the first Sunday of each month

This museum houses Portugal's most important collection of ancient art, featuring works by Portuguese and European masters, including paintings, sculptures, and decorative arts. The beautiful gardens also provide a lovely spot to relax.

2. Museu Calouste Gulbenkian

Address: Av. de Berna 45 A, 1067-001 Lisbon

Entry Fee: €10 for adults; free for under 18 and on Sundays

This museum showcases an extensive collection of Eastern and Western art, ranging from ancient artifacts to modern masterpieces. The surrounding park is perfect for a leisurely stroll.

3. MAAT (Museum of Art, Architecture and Technology)

Address: Av. Brasília, Central Tejo, 1400-038 Lisbon

Entry Fee: €9 for adults; free for under 18 and on the first Sunday of each month

Located along the river, MAAT combines contemporary art with innovative architecture. Its exhibitions focus on the intersection of art, technology, and sustainability.

4. Museu do Fado

Address: Largo do Chafariz de Dentro, 1, 1100-139 Lisbon
Entry Fee: €5 for adults; free for under 12
Dedicated to Fado, Portugal's soulful music genre, this museum explores the history and cultural significance of Fado through exhibits and audio-visual installations.

Historical Sites in Lisbon:

Lisbon's historical sites are a testament to its rich heritage and architectural beauty.

1. Belém Tower (Torre de Belém)

Address: Av. Brasília, 1400-038 Lisbon
Entry Fee: €6 for adults; free for under 12
This UNESCO World Heritage site, built in the 16th century, served as a fortress and part of the maritime defense system. Visitors can explore its intricate architecture and enjoy views of the Tagus River.

2. Jerónimos Monastery (Mosteiro dos Jerónimos)

Address: Praça do Império 1400-206 Lisbon

Entry Fee: €10 for adults; free for under 12

Another UNESCO World Heritage site, this monastery is a masterpiece of Manueline architecture. Its stunning cloisters and church are well worth a visit, reflecting Portugal's Age of Discoveries.

3. Praça do Comércio

Address: Praça do Comércio, 1100-148 Lisbon

Entry Fee: Free

This iconic square by the Tagus River is surrounded by impressive arches and is a central hub for locals and tourists alike. It's an excellent spot for photos and to enjoy a meal at one of the nearby restaurants.

4. Castelo de São Jorge (St. George's Castle)

Address: R. de Santa Cruz do Castelo, 1100-129 Lisbon

Entry Fee: €10 for adults; free for under 12

Perched atop a hill, this castle offers stunning panoramic views of the city. Explore its walls, towers, and archaeological site while immersing yourself in Lisbon's history.

Lisbon's museums and historical sites provide a captivating insight into the city's artistic heritage and rich past. From the ancient collections of the Museu Nacional de Arte Antiga to the stunning architecture of the Jerónimos Monastery, visitors can experience the essence of Lisbon's cultural identity. Each site reflects the city's evolution and offers memorable experiences for all who visit.

CHAPTER 4: COIMBRA

LUXURY HOTELS IN COIMBRA

Pestana Palace Coimbra

Price: From €150 per night

Address: Rua das Azenhas 2, 3000-192 Coimbra

A 5-star hotel set in a stunning 19th-century palace, offering luxurious accommodations with modern amenities. Enjoy breathtaking views of the Mondego River and beautiful gardens.

Quinta das Lágrimas

Price: From €140 per night

Address: Rua António Augusto Gonçalves, 3000-019 Coimbra

A luxurious hotel located in a historic estate, blending comfort with rich history. Guests can enjoy the beautiful gardens, a spa, and fine dining at the on-site restaurant.

Hotel D. Inês de Castro

Price: From €120 per night

Address: Av. de Lisboa, 3000-300 Coimbra

This elegant 4-star hotel is located near the city center, offering comfortable rooms, an outdoor pool, and stunning views of the city and river.

Vila Galé Coimbra

Price: From €110 per night

Address: Rua Abade Pedro, 3000-302 Coimbra

A contemporary hotel featuring spacious rooms, a spa, and an outdoor swimming pool. It's conveniently located near major attractions in Coimbra.

TOP 4 MID-RANGE AND LOW BUDGET STAYS IN COIMBRA

Hotel Oslo

Price: From €80 per night

Address: Rua 1º de Maio, 3000-300 Coimbra

A cozy mid-range hotel with comfortable rooms, offering a complimentary breakfast and located just a short walk from the city's attractions.

Ibis Coimbra

Price: From €70 per night

Address: Av. Armando Gonçalves 20, 3000-044 Coimbra

A budget-friendly hotel known for its modern amenities, comfortable rooms, and convenient location, making it perfect for travelers looking for affordability without sacrificing quality.

Casa Pombal

Price: From €60 per night

Address: Rua Pombal 5, 3000-330 Coimbra

A charming guesthouse offering a homey atmosphere and well-furnished rooms. Its central location provides easy access to local attractions.

Almedina Coimbra Centro

Price: From €50 per night

Address: Rua da Liberdade 56, 3000-123 Coimbra

An affordable option with clean and comfortable rooms. Located near the historical center, it's ideal for budget travelers who want to explore Coimbra.

WHERE TO EAT IN COIMBRA

Restaurante Loggia

Price: €30-€50 per person

Address: Rua Larga, 3000-248 Coimbra

Located within the Machado de Castro National Museum, this restaurant offers a refined dining experience with spectacular views and a menu that features contemporary interpretations of traditional Portuguese dishes.

Zé Manel dos Ossos

Price: €15-€25 per person

Address: Rua Quebra Costas 17, 3000-339 Coimbra

A local favorite, this informal eatery serves authentic regional dishes in a cozy atmosphere. Known for its friendly service and hearty portions.

A Tasquinha

Price: €20-€35 per person

Address: Rua da Figueira 25, 3000-202 Coimbra

A charming restaurant that specializes in traditional Portuguese cuisine, particularly known for its delectable meat dishes and excellent service.

Restaurante O Trovador

Price: €15-€30 per person

Address: Rua da Figueira 16, 3000-201 Coimbra

A delightful spot offering a range of Portuguese tapas and grilled dishes, with a warm and welcoming ambiance perfect for casual dining.

COFFEE AND CAFÉ SHOPS IN COIMBRA

A Brasileira

Price: €4-€8 per coffee/snack

Address: Rua Ferreira Borges 90, 3000-200 Coimbra

A historic café with a charming atmosphere, perfect for enjoying a coffee and pastry while taking in the local vibe and history.

Café Santa Cruz

Price: €3-€7 per coffee/snack

Address: Praça 8 de Maio, 3000-300 Coimbra

A beautiful café located in a former church, serving coffee, light meals, and pastries. Its lovely interior and outdoor seating make it a great spot to relax.

Café de São Francisco

Price: €3-€6 per coffee/snack

Address: Rua da Ilha 2, 3000-205 Coimbra

A quaint café known for its friendly staff and cozy ambiance, offering delicious coffee and light snacks, making it a favorite among locals and students.

Café A Caverna

Price: €2-€5 per coffee/snack

Address: Rua Pedro Monteiro 28, 3000-253 Coimbra

A unique, underground café with a relaxed atmosphere, perfect for a quick coffee break or studying while enjoying a light snack.

BARS, NIGHTLIFE, AND ENTERTAINMENT IN COIMBRA

Bar da Praça

Price: €5-€15 per drink

Address: Praça 8 de Maio, 3000-300 Coimbra

A vibrant bar with a lively atmosphere, offering a great selection of drinks and a perfect place to mingle with locals and fellow travelers.

Café Toga

Price: €4-€10 per drink

Address: Rua da Sota 12, 3000-336 Coimbra

A trendy bar known for its cocktails and relaxed vibe, making it a popular spot for both locals and students.

MusicBox Coimbra

Price: €10-€20 per event

Address: Rua do Tatu 5, 3000-124 Coimbra

A unique venue hosting live music and events, featuring a mix of genres. It's an excellent place to experience Coimbra's nightlife and music scene.

Pérola Negra

Price: €5-€15 per drink

Address: Rua da Sofia 19, 3000-390 Coimbra

A lively bar known for its eclectic decor and vibrant atmosphere, perfect for enjoying a drink and dancing the night away.

Museums and Galleries in Coimbra

Coimbra, one of Portugal's oldest cities, is renowned for its rich cultural heritage and vibrant arts scene. Visitors can explore several noteworthy museums and galleries that highlight its historical significance and artistic contributions.

1. Joanina Library (Biblioteca Joanina)

Address: Largo da Porta Férrea, 3000-270 Coimbra

Entry Fee: €12; free for students and staff of the University of Coimbra

The Joanina Library, part of the University of Coimbra, is a stunning Baroque masterpiece. Founded in the 18th century, it houses an impressive collection of over 200,000 books. The library's ornate interior features beautiful wooden shelves and gilded decorations, making it one of the most beautiful libraries in the world.

2. National Museum Machado de Castro

Address: R. de Ferreira Borges, 3000-200 Coimbra

Entry Fee: €6 for adults; free for under-18s

Housed in a former bishop's palace, this museum showcases a rich collection of Portuguese art from the Roman period to the 19th century. Highlights include works by renowned sculptor Machado de Castro and stunning Roman artifacts, including the Mosaic of the Labyrinth.

3. Museu da Ciência da Universidade de Coimbra

Address: Rua Larga, 3000-117 Coimbra

Entry Fee: €4 for adults; free for children under 12

The Museum of Science offers engaging exhibits focusing on the history of science and education in Portugal. It features a variety of interactive displays, historical scientific instruments, and a rich collection of botanical and geological specimens.

4. Arco de Almedina

Address: R. da Almedina, 3000-202 Coimbra

Entry Fee: Free

This medieval archway, once part of Coimbra's ancient city walls, offers insights into the city's history. Visitors can walk through and explore the surrounding historical district.

Historical Sites in Coimbra

Coimbra is dotted with significant historical sites that reflect its glorious past and cultural richness.

1. University of Coimbra (Universidade de Coimbra)

Address: Paço das Escolas, 3000-240 Coimbra

Entry Fee: €12 for adults; reduced rates for students and groups

Established in 1290, the University of Coimbra is one of the oldest universities in Europe. The campus features stunning architecture, including the Royal Palace, the Mathematical Tower, and the Botanical Garden, making it a UNESCO World Heritage site.

2. Coimbra Cathedral (Sé Velha)

Address: Largo da Sé Velha, 3000-213 Coimbra

Entry Fee: €4 for adults

This Romanesque cathedral dates back to the 12th century and features impressive stonework and ornate altars. Its cloister is also notable for its beautiful Manueline-style architecture.

3. Santa Clara-a-Velha Monastery

Address: Av. de Emídio Navarro, 3000-304 Coimbra

Entry Fee: €4 for adults; free for under-18s

The Santa Clara-a-Velha monastery is a stunning example of Gothic architecture. The site, now partially in ruins, was once home to a community of nuns and is set along the banks of the Mondego River. The adjoining museum showcases artifacts from the monastery's history.

4. Portugal dos Pequenitos

Address: R. do Brasil, 3000-333 Coimbra

Entry Fee: €8 for adults; discounts for children

This miniature park features scaled-down replicas of Portugal's most famous monuments and is an engaging way to learn about the country's architectural heritage. It's especially fun for families and children.

Coimbra's museums and historical sites offer a fascinating glimpse into the city's rich cultural and artistic heritage. From the exquisite Joanina Library to the ancient walls of the University of Coimbra, visitors will find a wealth of knowledge and beauty that speaks to the heart of Portugal's past.

CHAPTER 5: WHAT TO DO IN PORTUGAL

Portugal offers an array of experiences for visitors, from stunning beaches to lively festivals, outdoor activities, and opportunities to make friends with locals. Whether you're drawn to the history, the natural beauty, or the rich cultural heritage, there's something for everyone.

FESTIVALS TO PARTICIPATE IN

Portugal is known for its vibrant festivals, many of which offer a glimpse into the country's rich cultural and religious heritage. These celebrations, which often combine music, dance, food, and religious processions, provide visitors with an opportunity to engage deeply with local traditions.

Carnaval (February/March)

Held in various towns across Portugal, especially in Torres Vedras, Ovar, and Madeira.

Similar to Brazil's Carnival, Portugal's version is a vibrant celebration of parades, costumes, and music. Visitors can dress up, join the street parties, and experience the festive atmosphere.

Festa de São João (June 23-24)

Porto

One of Portugal's most famous festivals, Festa de São João celebrates St. John with fireworks, street dancing, and feasting. The unique tradition of hitting people with plastic hammers adds a playful touch to the event. Don't miss the grilled sardines served along the Douro River.

Festas dos Santos Populares (June)

Lisbon

This month-long celebration honors Lisbon's patron saint, Santo António. The streets are filled with parades, music, and grilled sardines, with festivities taking place in popular neighborhoods like Alfama, Bica, and Bairro Alto.

Festa da Ria Formosa (August)

Faro

This seafood festival is a must for seafood lovers. It celebrates the region's culinary traditions with a focus on the local shellfish, all while offering live music and entertainment.

Festa da Flor (April/May)

Madeira

A celebration of spring, the Flower Festival fills the streets of Funchal with vibrant parades, intricate flower carpets, and displays. This colorful festival is a photographer's dream and celebrates the beauty of Madeira's flora.

Participating in these festivals allows visitors to connect with locals, understand Portuguese culture on a deeper level, and immerse themselves in the joyous spirit that defines Portuguese celebrations.

OUTDOOR ACTIVITIES

Portugal's natural landscapes are ideal for outdoor enthusiasts. Whether you prefer the mountains, the sea, or the countryside, there are plenty of opportunities to explore the great outdoors.

Water Sports

Surfing

Portugal is one of Europe's top surfing destinations, with renowned spots like Nazaré, known for its giant waves, and

Ericeira, a World Surfing Reserve. Surfing schools are plentiful, offering lessons for beginners and seasoned surfers alike.

Kayaking

Explore Portugal's rivers and coastlines by kayak. The Douro River, for example, offers serene kayaking experiences through its valleys, while the Algarve's coast is famous for kayaking along its limestone caves and grottoes, especially at Ponta da Piedade in Lagos.

Beach Sports

Beach Volleyball

Many of Portugal's beaches, particularly in the Algarve and Lisbon regions, have areas designated for beach volleyball. Joining a casual game is a great way to meet locals and fellow travelers while staying active.

Engaging in outdoor activities not only allows you to experience Portugal's natural beauty but also to bond with fellow adventurers, both local and international.

Yoga and Wellness Retreats

Portugal is fast becoming a destination for those seeking relaxation and wellness. Yoga retreats are available across the country, from the serene beaches of the Algarve to the tranquil countryside of Alentejo.

Monte Velho Eco Retreat (Algarve)

Address: Monte Velho, Carrapateira, Algarve

Monte Velho is a peaceful retreat center surrounded by nature, offering yoga, meditation, and holistic therapies. With ocean views and nearby beaches, it's the perfect spot for relaxation and rejuvenation.

Surya Yoga Retreats (Ericeira)

Address: 2640 Mafra, Lisbon District

Ericeira, known for its surf culture, also hosts several yoga retreats. Surya Yoga blends yoga and surfing, providing a balance of physical activity and relaxation, making it a top choice for health-conscious visitors.

Vale de Moses (Castelo Branco)

Address: Amieira, Oleiros, Castelo Branco District

Nestled in the mountains of central Portugal, Vale de Moses offers immersive yoga retreats that focus on mindfulness, healing, and connecting with nature. It's a perfect spot to unwind from the stresses of daily life.

Yoga and wellness retreats in Portugal offer visitors the chance to unplug, practice mindfulness, and restore balance in their lives. These retreats are also excellent places to meet like-minded travelers and form lasting friendships.

PORTUGAL LOCAL CUISINE TO TRY

Portugal's diverse regions offer a wide variety of local cuisines that are both flavorful and deeply rooted in tradition. If you're visiting the country, here are ten iconic Portuguese dishes you must try:

1. Bacalhau à Brás (Codfish à Brás)

A beloved Portuguese dish, Bacalhau à Brás is a comforting blend of shredded salted cod, onions, and finely chopped potatoes, all bound together with scrambled eggs. Garnished with parsley and olives, this dish is a staple across Portugal. Best Place to Try: Lisbon

2. Caldo Verde (Green Soup)

One of Portugal's most famous soups, Caldo Verde is made with thinly sliced kale, potatoes, onions, and garlic, all blended into a smooth, hearty broth. It is often served with slices of chorizo (smoked sausage) and enjoyed with crusty bread. Best Place to Try: Northern Portugal, especially in Minho

3. Sardinhas Assadas (Grilled Sardines)

A quintessential summer dish, grilled sardines are especially popular during the Santo António festival in Lisbon. These fresh sardines are grilled to perfection, seasoned with coarse salt, and typically served with boiled potatoes or a simple salad. Best Place to Try: Lisbon and coastal towns like Porto

4. Pastéis de Nata (Custard Tarts)

These iconic Portuguese custard tarts have a flaky, buttery crust filled with creamy custard and topped with a light dusting of cinnamon or powdered sugar. They are best enjoyed with a coffee. Best Place to Try: Pastéis de Belém in Lisbon

5. Arroz de Marisco (Seafood Rice)

Arroz de Marisco is a rich, flavorful dish made with various seafood like shrimp, clams, and mussels cooked in a saffron-infused rice broth. This Portuguese seafood stew is reminiscent of Spain's paella but with its unique twist. Best Place to Try: Setúbal or the coastal regions of the Algarve

6. Leitão da Bairrada (Roast Suckling Pig)

Leitão da Bairrada is a delicacy from the Bairrada region, where the pig is slowly roasted until the skin is crisp and golden, while the meat remains tender. It is often served with potatoes, orange slices, and a crisp salad. Best Place to Try: Bairrada, near Coimbra

7. Amêijoas à Bulhão Pato (Clams Bulhão Pato Style)

This simple yet flavorful dish consists of fresh clams steamed in garlic, olive oil, coriander, and white wine. It is a common appetizer or petisco (small plate) and is perfect when paired with crusty bread to soak up the broth. Best Place to Try: Algarve and Lisbon

8. Alheira de Mirandela (Smoked Sausage)

Alheira is a unique Portuguese sausage made with bread and a mixture of meats like poultry, veal, and pork, often served fried with potatoes and eggs. This dish has historical significance, as it was created by Jews during the Inquisition to appear as if they were eating pork. Best Place to Try: Trás-os-Montes, Northern Portugal

9. Polvo à Lagareiro (Octopus with Olive Oil and Garlic)

This traditional dish features tender octopus baked with generous amounts of olive oil, garlic, and herbs, typically served with roasted potatoes. It's one of the most beloved seafood dishes in Portugal. Best Place to Try: Porto and coastal towns in the north

10. Queijo da Serra (Serra Cheese)

This creamy, rich cheese comes from the Serra da Estrela mountains and is made from sheep's milk. It's often served as an appetizer with bread or as a dessert with jams and honey. The texture varies from semi-soft to runny, depending on its aging process. Best Place to Try: Serra da Estrela region

These iconic dishes highlight the rich diversity of Portugal's regional culinary traditions.

BEACHES TO EXPLORE

Portugal is home to some of the most beautiful beaches in Europe, many of which are situated along its stunning Atlantic coastline.

Praia da Marinha (Algarve)

Address: Estr. de Benagil, 8400 Lagoa

Known for its dramatic cliffs, clear waters, and golden sand, Praia da Marinha is consistently ranked as one of the most beautiful beaches in Portugal. It's perfect for sunbathing, swimming, and snorkeling.

Praia do Guincho (Cascais)

Address: Estrada do Guincho, 2750-642 Cascais

This expansive beach is famous for its strong winds, making it a popular spot for windsurfing and kite surfing. Its natural beauty and proximity to Lisbon make it a favorite for day trips.

Praia da Rocha (Portimão)

Address: Av. Tomás Cabreira, 8500-802 Portimão

Praia da Rocha is one of the Algarve's largest and most popular beaches. Its wide sandy expanse is lined with vibrant beach bars and restaurants, making it ideal for both relaxation and socializing.

Praia de Carcavelos (Cascais)

Address: Avenida Marginal, Carcavelos

Located just outside Lisbon, Praia de Carcavelos is a lively beach frequented by both locals and tourists. With good surf, beach volleyball courts, and plenty of food options, it's a great place for an active day at the beach.

Each beach in Portugal offers its own unique atmosphere, from tranquil coves to bustling beach bars. Visitors are encouraged to explore as many as possible during their stay.

5. Local Sports and Games

Portugal is passionate about sports, and visitors can join in on the excitement. Whether it's playing football, trying traditional games, or watching local competitions, there are plenty of opportunities to get involved.

Football (Soccer)

Football is by far the most popular sport in Portugal. Visitors can watch matches in local stadiums or even join informal games in parks and on beaches. Attending a match at Lisbon's Estádio da Luz or Porto's Estádio do Dragão is an unforgettable experience.

Petanca (Bocce)

Petanca is a popular game in Portugal, especially in the southern regions. It's similar to bocce, where players throw metal balls to get them as close as possible to a smaller target ball. Visitors are often welcomed to join local games in parks.

Surfing Competitions

Portugal hosts world-class surfing competitions, such as the MEO Rip Curl Pro Portugal in Peniche. Even if you're not a surfer, attending these competitions offers a thrilling look into Portugal's surf culture.

Participating in or watching local sports allows visitors to engage with the community and experience the excitement that sports bring to Portuguese life.

Making Friends in Portugal

One of the most rewarding aspects of visiting Portugal is the opportunity to make friends with locals. The Portuguese are known for their warm hospitality, and forming connections can lead to a deeper, more meaningful travel experience.

Join Local Events and Festivals: Festivals are a great way to meet people. Don't be afraid to strike up a conversation with locals during these lively events. The Portuguese are proud of their traditions and are often happy to share stories and tips about their country.

Attend Language Exchange Meetups: In larger cities like Lisbon and Porto, language exchange meetups are common. These gatherings are an excellent opportunity for visitors to practice Portuguese and meet locals eager to improve their English or other languages.

Participate in Group Activities: From yoga classes to hiking groups, participating in group activities helps visitors' bond with locals over shared interests. Platforms like Meetup or local Facebook groups can be great resources for finding events.

Frequent Local Cafés and Bars: Spend time in local cafés or bars to observe the local way of life. Engaging with staff or other patrons is an easy and organic way to build connections in a relaxed environment.

Portugal offers a wide variety of experiences that go beyond sightseeing. From attending traditional festivals and participating in local outdoor activities to relaxing on stunning beaches and making friends, Portugal promises a deeply enriching travel experience.

HIKING AND WALKING TRAIL IN PORTUGAL

Portugal offers some of the most beautiful and diverse hiking trails in Europe, from coastal paths with stunning ocean views to mountain treks through ancient forests and villages. Whether you're an experienced hiker or a casual walker, the country's well-marked trails and varied landscapes provide plenty of opportunities to explore on foot. Here are some of the best hiking and walking trails in Portugal, showcasing the natural beauty and cultural richness of the country.

1. Rota Vicentina (Alentejo and Algarve)

- Location: Southwest Coast, from Santiago do Cacém to Cape St. Vincent
- Length: Over 400 kilometers
- Difficulty: Moderate to challenging, with shorter sections for beginners
- Entry: Free

The Rota Vicentina is one of Portugal's most iconic long-distance hiking routes, stretching along the beautiful southwestern coast.

The trail offers two main routes: the Historical Way, which takes you through rural villages and farmlands, and the Fishermen's Trail, which follows the rugged coastline with breathtaking views of cliffs and secluded beaches. The Fishermen's Trail, in particular, offers some of the most scenic coastal hiking in Europe, while the Historical Way immerses you in the traditional way of life in the Alentejo countryside. Hikers can choose to tackle the entire route or just select sections, depending on their time and fitness level.

2. Peneda-Gerês National Park (Northern Portugal)

- Location: Peneda-Gerês National Park, northern Portugal
- Length: Various trails ranging from short walks to multi-day hikes
- Difficulty: Easy to challenging
- Entry: Free, some parking fees at main sites

Peneda-Gerês National Park, Portugal's only national park, is a paradise for nature lovers. This remote and wild region offers numerous hiking trails that lead you through lush forests, past crystal-clear rivers, and to stunning viewpoints. One of the most popular routes is the Trilho dos Currais, a circular route that offers panoramic views of the park's dramatic landscapes, including towering mountains and ancient Roman roads. The Mezio-Geres Trail is another well-known hike that takes you through waterfalls and oak forests. The park is also home to wildlife such as wild horses, deer, and eagles, adding to the magic of this natural wonder.

3. Paiva Walkways (Arouca)

- Location: Arouca, north-central Portugal
- Length: 8 kilometers
- Difficulty: Moderate
- Entry: €2-€5 (varies by season)

The Paiva Walkways (Passadiços do Paiva) offer an exhilarating hike along wooden boardwalks that follow the course of the Paiva River. This trail is renowned for its dramatic scenery, passing through rugged cliffs, waterfalls, and crystal-clear river pools. The walk is both thrilling and scenic, with suspension bridges that offer breathtaking views of the surrounding landscape. It's perfect for families, nature enthusiasts, and those who enjoy a blend of adventure and relaxation. The walkways also offer educational signage about the area's rich biodiversity and geology, making it an informative experience as well.

4. Madeira Levada Walks

- Location: Madeira Island
- Length: Various, from short walks to multi-day hikes
- Difficulty: Easy to moderate
- Entry: Free

Madeira is famous for its levadas, ancient irrigation channels that snake through the island's mountainous terrain, and these form the backbone of many of its best hiking trails. The Levada do Caldeirão Verde is one of the most popular, taking you on a scenic journey through lush Laurisilva forests to the spectacular Caldeirão Verde waterfall. Another favorite is the Levada do Rei, which offers stunning views of the island's dramatic landscapes and vibrant flora. These hikes are generally easy to moderate, making them suitable for walkers of all abilities. Along the way, you'll be treated to breathtaking vistas of Madeira's rugged cliffs, deep valleys, and dramatic coastline.

5. Serra da Estrela (Central Portugal)

- Location: Serra da Estrela Natural Park, Central Portugal
- Length: Various trails, ranging from short hikes to multi-day treks
- Difficulty: Moderate to challenging
- Entry: Free

The Serra da Estrela mountain range is the highest in mainland Portugal and offers some of the most exhilarating hiking in the country. Its trails take you through rugged, rocky landscapes, glacial valleys, and peaceful mountain villages. One of the most famous hikes is the Torre trek, which leads you to the highest point in mainland Portugal at 1,993 meters. Along the way, you'll encounter glacial lagoons, ancient shepherd huts, and spectacular vistas over the surrounding countryside. In winter, the region transforms into a skiing and snowboarding destination, but during the warmer months, it's perfect for hiking.

6. Douro Valley Vineyards

- Location: Douro Valley, Northern Portugal
- Length: Various vineyard trails
- Difficulty: Easy to moderate
- Entry: Free or part of vineyard tours (prices vary)

For those who want to combine hiking with wine tasting, the Douro Valley is the perfect destination. This UNESCO World Heritage site is famous for its terraced vineyards that produce Portugal's renowned port wine. There are several trails that wind through the vineyards, offering stunning views of the Douro River and the surrounding countryside. Many of the hikes include stops at local quintas (wineries), where you can sample some of the region's finest wines. The São Leonardo da Galafura viewpoint is a popular stop, offering sweeping vistas over the valley's dramatic landscape.

7. Sintra-Cascais Natural Park

- Location: Sintra-Cascais Natural Park, near Lisbon
- Length: Various trails, from short walks to full-day hikes
- Difficulty: Easy to moderate
- Entry: Free, some fees for specific sites (such as Pena Palace)

Just a short drive from Lisbon, the Sintra-Cascais Natural Park is a magical area of lush forests, palaces, and coastline. One of the most popular hikes is the Caminho das Vinhas, which takes you through the forested hills of Sintra to the stunning Pena Palace and Castle of the Moors. If you're seeking coastal views, the trail from Cabo da Roca, the westernmost point of mainland Europe, offers dramatic cliffs and sweeping ocean vistas. The combination of history, nature, and spectacular views makes this region a hiker's dream.

8. Azores Walking Trails

- Location: Azores Islands, mid-Atlantic
- Length: Various, from short walks to multi-day hikes
- Difficulty: Easy to challenging
- Entry: Free

The Azores archipelago is a hiker's paradise, with its volcanic landscapes, crater lakes, and lush green forests. The Sete Cidades trail on São Miguel Island is one of the most famous, offering breathtaking views of the twin blue and green lakes that fill an ancient volcanic crater. Another highlight is the Pico Mountain hike, which takes you to the summit of Portugal's highest peak at 2,351 meters. The island of Flores offers stunning coastal walks, where you can explore waterfalls and pristine beaches, while the Furnas Valley is known for its geothermal hot springs and unique landscape.

9. Algarve Coastal Trails

- Location: Algarve, southern Portugal
- Length: Various coastal trails
- Difficulty: Easy to moderate
- Entry: Free

The Algarve is famous for its golden beaches and dramatic cliffs, and there are numerous coastal trails that allow hikers to explore this stunning region on foot. The Seven Hanging Valleys Trail is one of the most popular, taking you along the clifftops between Praia da Marinha and Praia de Vale Centeanes. The trail offers stunning views of sea caves, hidden beaches, and the rugged coastline. Another favorite is the Ponta da Piedade trail in Lagos, which leads you along the cliffs to some of the Algarve's most iconic rock formations and sea arches.

10. Monserrate Palace and Gardens (Sintra)

- Location: Sintra, Lisbon District
- Length: Short, scenic garden walks
- Difficulty: Easy
- Entry: €7.50 for adults

Although not a traditional hike, the gardens surrounding the Monserrate Palace in Sintra offer some of the most beautiful walking paths in Portugal. The exotic gardens, filled with rare plants and flowers from around the world, are a peaceful place to explore on foot. The palace itself is a stunning example of Romantic architecture, and the walking trails provide fantastic views of the surrounding forest and mountains.

Portugal's hiking and walking trails offer something for every type of outdoor enthusiast. Whether you're seeking challenging mountain treks, scenic coastal paths, or relaxing strolls through vineyards and forests, Portugal's diverse landscapes provide endless opportunities to explore. With a combination of natural beauty, cultural landmarks, and welcoming local communities, hiking in Portugal is a rewarding way to experience the country's rich heritage and stunning scenery.

Portuguese language to interact with the local

Here's a list of basic Portuguese phrases that can help you interact with locals in various situations, along with their pronunciations:

Greetings

- **Hello**

    Portuguese: Olá

    Pronunciation: oh-LAH

- **Good morning**

    Portuguese: Bom dia

    Pronunciation: bohm DEE-ah

- **Good afternoon**

    Portuguese: Boa tarde

    Pronunciation: BOH-ah TAR-deh

- **Good evening**

    Portuguese: Boa noite

    Pronunciation: BOH-ah NOY-teh

- **How are you?**

    Portuguese: Como você está?

    Pronunciation: KOH-moh voh-SEH es-TAH?

Basic Conversations

- **Please**

    Portuguese: Por favor

    Pronunciation: por fah-VOR

- **Thank you (male) / Thank you (female)**

    Portuguese: Obrigado (male) / Obrigada (female)

Pronunciation: oh-bree-GAH-doh / oh-bree-GAH-dah

➢ **You're welcome**

Portuguese: De nada

Pronunciation: jeh NAH-dah

➢ **Excuse me**

Portuguese: Com licença

Pronunciation: kohm lee-SEN-sah

➢ **I'm sorry**

Portuguese: Desculpe

Pronunciation: des-KOOL-peh

Directions and Assistance

➢ **Where is...?**

Portuguese: Onde fica...?

Pronunciation: OHN-deh FEE-kah...?

➢ **Can you help me?**

Portuguese: Você pode me ajudar?

Pronunciation: voh-SEH POH-jee meh ah-zhoo-DAR?

➢ **How much does this cost?**

Portuguese: Quanto custa isto?

Pronunciation: KWAN-toh KOOS-tah EES-toh?

Dining and Shopping

- I would like...

    Portuguese: Eu gostaria de...

    Pronunciation: eh-oo goh-stah-REE-ah jee...

- The bill, please

    Portuguese: A conta, por favor

    Pronunciation: ah KOHN-tah, por fah-VOR

- Do you have vegetarian options?

    Portuguese: Você tem opções vegetarianas?

    Pronunciation: voh-SEH taym op-SYOH-ees veh-zhee-tah-REE-ah-nahs?

Casual Interactions

- What is your name?

    Portuguese: Qual é o seu nome?

    Pronunciation: KWAHL eh oo SEH-oo NOH-mee?

- My name is...

    Portuguese: Meu nome é...

    Pronunciation: MEH-oo NOH-mee eh...

- Nice to meet you

    Portuguese: Prazer em conhecê-lo / conhecê-la

    Pronunciation: prah-ZER eng koh-nyay-SEH-loh / koh-nyay-SEH-lah

> **Goodbye**

  Portuguese: Adeus

  Pronunciation: ah-DEH-ooz

Emergency Phrases

> **I need help!**

  Portuguese: Eu preciso de ajuda!

  Pronunciation: eh-oo preh-ZEE-zoo jee ah-ZHOO-dah!

> **Call the police!**

  Portuguese: Chame a polícia!

  Pronunciation: SHA-meh ah poh-LEE-see-ah!

> **I feel sick**

  Portuguese: Eu me sinto doente

  Pronunciation: eh-oo mee SEEN-toh do-EHN-chee

These phrases will help you navigate different situations while interacting with locals in Portugal. Enjoy your trip!

CHAPTER 6: 7 DAYS ITINERARY IN PORTUGAL

Here's a 7-day itinerary for exploring Portugal, covering its vibrant cities, stunning landscapes, and rich culture.

Day 1: Arrival in Lisbon

Morning: Arrive in Lisbon, check into your hotel.

Afternoon: Explore Alfama, the oldest district in Lisbon. Visit Lisbon Cathedral and enjoy the stunning views from the Miradouro de Santa Luzia.

Evening: Dinner at a local restaurant. Try Bacalhau à Brás (codfish) and enjoy live Fado music in Alfama.

Day 2: Lisbon City Exploration

Morning: Visit the Belém district. Explore the Jerónimos Monastery (entry fee: €10) and the Tower of Belém (entry fee: €6). Don't forget to try a Pastel de Belém at the famous bakery.

Afternoon: Head to the MAAT (Museum of Art, Architecture and Technology). Entry fee: €9.

Evening: Enjoy dinner in the Bairro Alto district. Try Petiscos (Portuguese tapas).

Day 3: Sintra Day Trip

Morning: Take a train to Sintra (approx. 40 minutes). Visit the Pena Palace (entry fee: €14) and explore its colorful architecture and gardens.

Afternoon: Visit the Quinta da Regaleira (entry fee: €10) and its magical gardens and initiation well.

Evening: Return to Lisbon and enjoy dinner at a local restaurant.

Day 4: Lisbon to Porto

Morning: Take a train from Lisbon to Porto (approx. 3 hours). Check into your hotel.

Afternoon: Explore the Ribeira district. Walk along the Douro River and visit the iconic Dom Luís I Bridge.

Evening: Dinner at a riverside restaurant. Try Francesinha, a hearty sandwich typical of Porto.

Day 5: Porto City Exploration

Morning: Visit the Livraria Lello, one of the most beautiful bookstores in the world (entry fee: €5). Then, explore the Clérigos Tower (entry fee: €6) for panoramic views of the city.

Afternoon: Visit the São Bento Railway Station to admire its stunning azulejos (blue tiles). Then, tour the Palácio da Bolsa (entry fee: €10).

Evening: Enjoy a wine tasting at one of the many Port wine cellars in Vila Nova de Gaia.

Day 6: Douro Valley Day Trip

Morning: Take a scenic drive or join a guided tour to the Douro Valley, famous for its terraced vineyards.

Afternoon: Enjoy a river cruise along the Douro River, stopping at a vineyard for wine tasting and lunch (approx. €25-€50).

Evening: Return to Porto for dinner. Enjoy local seafood dishes.

Day 7: Departure from Porto

Morning: Visit the Serralves Museum, which showcases contemporary art and beautiful gardens (entry fee: €10).

Afternoon: Last-minute shopping in Porto or explore any remaining sights.

Evening: Depart from Porto or return to Lisbon if your flight is from there.

CHAPTER 7: HEALTH AND SAFETY RULES

Traveling to Spain and Portugal can be an exhilarating experience filled with rich culture, beautiful landscapes, and warm hospitality. However, it is essential to prioritize safety and health etiquette, especially for older travelers or those unsure about their health while navigating new environments. Below are some valuable tips to ensure a safe and enjoyable visit to these vibrant countries.

Health Etiquette and General Advice

Consult Your Doctor: Before embarking on your journey, it is crucial to consult your healthcare provider, especially if you have pre-existing health conditions. Discuss any necessary vaccinations or medications you may need during your trip.

Don't forget Travel Insurance: Purchase travel insurance that covers health emergencies, including hospital stays, medication, and evacuation if necessary. This provides peace of mind, especially for older travelers who may require medical assistance.

Stay Hydrated: Spain and Portugal can be hot, especially during summer months. Drink plenty of water to stay hydrated, and avoid excessive alcohol consumption, which can lead to dehydration. Always carry a refillable water bottle to keep yourself hydrated throughout the day.

Pace Yourself: Traveling can be physically demanding. For older travelers, it's essential to pace yourself and take breaks. Avoid overexertion by planning your itinerary with rest periods. Include leisurely activities and allow time to recharge.

Eat Healthily: Enjoying local cuisine is one of the highlights of traveling. However, be mindful of what you eat, especially if you have dietary restrictions or food allergies. Always communicate your dietary needs when dining out, and opt for balanced meals to maintain your energy levels.

Health Care Accessibility: Familiarize yourself with local healthcare facilities, including hospitals and pharmacies. In Spain, public health services are available to travelers with a European Health Insurance Card (EHIC), while Portugal offers emergency services through 112.

Spain and Portugal for Aged 60 and Above

Know Your Limits: Understand your physical limits and avoid activities that may be too strenuous. Choose guided tours that cater to older adults, as they are often designed to accommodate various fitness levels.

Comfortable Footwear: Invest in comfortable, supportive footwear suitable for walking. Many cities in Spain and Portugal have cobblestone streets and uneven terrain, making sturdy shoes essential for safety and comfort.

Rest and Relaxation: Allow for downtime during your trip. Find cafes or parks where you can sit and enjoy the ambiance. This not only helps to recharge your energy but also provides opportunities to meet locals and fellow travelers.

Emergency Contacts: Keep a list of emergency contacts, including your country's embassy, local hospitals, and family members. Having this information readily available can be invaluable in case of an emergency.

Join Group Tours: Consider joining group tours designed for seniors. These tours often include accessible transportation and allow for socializing with fellow travelers, enhancing your travel experience.

Retreat back to your accommodations if you notice a chance in your body system or when you get tired

Safety Etiquette While Exploring Tourist Attractions

Be Aware of Your Surroundings: Stay alert in crowded tourist areas, where pickpockets may operate. Keep your belongings close and be cautious when using your phone or taking photos.

Follow Local Laws and Customs: Familiarize yourself with the local laws and customs of Spain and Portugal. For example, it's illegal to drink alcohol in public places in certain areas, and respecting local traditions shows appreciation for the culture.

Keep Important Documents Safe: Make copies of your passport, travel insurance, and other important documents. Store them separately from the originals. Consider using a money belt or neck pouch for extra security.

Transportation Safety: When using public transportation, stay vigilant and keep your belongings secure. If using taxis, opt for licensed ones and confirm the fare before starting your journey.

Hiking and Adventure Activities

Choose Suitable Trails: If you plan to hike, choose trails that match your fitness level. Research the trails beforehand and consider guided hiking tours, especially if you're unfamiliar with the area.

Wear Appropriate Gear: Dress appropriately for hiking, including breathable clothing, sturdy shoes, and sun protection (sunscreen, hats, and sunglasses). Carry a small backpack with water, snacks, and a first-aid kit.

Stay on Marked Paths: Always stick to marked trails to avoid getting lost and to protect the natural environment. Respect local wildlife and flora by not straying from designated paths.

Travel in Groups: When hiking or participating in adventure activities, it's safer to go in groups. This not only enhances safety but also allows for shared experiences and camaraderie.

Check Weather Conditions: Before setting out on any outdoor activities, check the weather forecast. Be prepared for sudden changes in weather, and carry appropriate gear to handle unexpected conditions.

Inform Someone of Your Plans: If you're going hiking or engaging in adventure activities, let someone know your itinerary and expected return time. This is especially important for solo travelers.

Traveling to Spain and Portugal can be an enriching experience when safety and health etiquette are prioritized. By taking necessary precautions, such as consulting a healthcare provider, purchasing travel insurance, and being aware of your surroundings, you can enjoy a safe and memorable journey. For older travelers, pacing yourself, choosing suitable activities, and being mindful of health needs will enhance the travel experience. Embrace the beauty and culture of these incredible countries while ensuring your health and safety come first.

CHAPTER 8: BONUS

Cost breakdown for different travel style

Planning a trip to Spain and Portugal involves considering various costs based on your travel style. Whether you're traveling on a low budget, mid-range, or luxury style, understanding the financial requirements is crucial for a smooth and enjoyable experience. Here's a detailed cost breakdown for a 7-day itinerary in Spain and Portugal, covering different travel styles: low budget, mid-range, and luxury.

1. Low Budget Travel Style

Traveling on a budget doesn't mean you have to miss out on the beauty and culture of Spain and Portugal. Here's how the costs break down for a week:

Accommodation
- Cost: €15 to €40 per night
- Total for 7 Nights:
- €105 to €280

Food
- Cost: €10 to €20 per day (inexpensive restaurants and street food)
- Total for 7 Days:

- €70 to €140

Transportation
- Cost: €5 to €10 per day (public transport)
- Total for 7 Days:
- €35 to €70

Attractions
- Cost: €5 to €15 per day (entry fees and free attractions)
- Total for 7 Days:
- €35 to €105

Local Activities
- Cost: €10 to €20 (e.g., yoga classes, local tours)
- Total:
- €10 to €20

Total Estimated Cost for Low Budget Travel Style
- Accommodation: €105 to €280
- Food: €70 to €140
- Transportation: €35 to €70
- Attractions: €35 to €105
- Local Activities: €10 to €20

Overall Total for 7 Days:

€355 to €615

2. Mid-Range Travel Style

If you're looking for a more comfortable experience, here's a breakdown of mid-range travel costs:

Accommodation
- Cost: €60 to €120 per night

- Total for 7 Nights:
- €420 to €840

Food

- Cost: €20 to €40 per day (casual dining)
- Total for 7 Days:
- €140 to €280

Transportation

- Cost: €10 to €20 per day (public transport and occasional taxis)
- Total for 7 Days:
- €70 to €140

Attractions

- Cost: €10 to €25 per day (popular attractions and guided tours)
- Total for 7 Days:
- €70 to €175

Local Activities

- Cost: €20 to €50 (e.g., workshops, cooking classes)
- Total:
- €20 to €50

Total Estimated Cost for Mid-Range Travel Style

- Accommodation: €420 to €840
- Food: €140 to €280
- Transportation: €70 to €140
- Attractions: €70 to €175
- Local Activities: €20 to €50

Overall Total for 7 Days:

€720 to €1,485

3. Luxury Travel Style

For those seeking a lavish experience, here's the breakdown for a luxury trip:

Accommodation
Cost: €150 to €300 per night
- Total for 7 Nights:
- €1,050 to €2,100

Food
- Cost: €50 to €100 per day (fine dining)
- Total for 7 Days:
- €350 to €700

Transportation
- Cost: €30 to €70 per day (private transfers and car rentals)
- Total for 7 Days:
- €210 to €490

Attractions
- Cost: €25 to €50 per day (premium experiences)
- Total for 7 Days:
- €175 to €350

Local Activities
- Cost: €50 to €100 (e.g., private tours, luxury spa experiences)
- Total:
- €350 to €700

Total Estimated Cost for Luxury Travel Style
- Accommodation: €1,050 to €2,100

- Food: €350 to €700
- Transportation: €210 to €490
- Attractions: €175 to €350
- Local Activities: €350 to €700
- Overall Total for 7 Days:
- €2,335 to €4,440

Summary of Total Costs for 7 Days

- Low Budget: €355 to €615 or more
- Mid-Range: €720 to €1,485
- Luxury: €2,335 to €4,440

When planning your trip, consider your travel style and budget. The above calculations should help you gauge how much cash to bring along for your adventure in Spain and Portugal. Whether you're a backpacker or seeking luxury, having a clear understanding of costs will enable you to enjoy your travels without financial stress. Remember to account for additional expenses like souvenirs, unexpected activities, and emergencies.

Bringing at least €2000 for a week-long trip is advisable if you're aiming for a mid-range experience, ensuring you can explore, dine, and enjoy your journey without financial limitations.

CONCLUSION

As we conclude this travel guide to Spain and Portugal, we hope you feel inspired and well-prepared for your upcoming adventure. These vibrant countries are rich in history, culture, and breathtaking landscapes, offering countless experiences that cater to every traveler's desires. Whether you choose to explore the bustling streets of Madrid, relax on the sun-soaked beaches of the Algarve, or savor the culinary delights of Barcelona, your journey promises to be unforgettable.

Traveling can be a transformative experience, and we hope this guide has equipped you with the knowledge and insights needed to make the most of your trip. From navigating local customs to discovering hidden gems, we trust you will find joy in every moment of your journey.

Thank you for taking the time to read this guide. We appreciate your interest in exploring the wonders of Spain and Portugal. Remember to keep an open mind and embrace the unique experiences each destination has to offer. Safe travels, and may your adventures be filled with laughter, discovery, and cherished memories! Enjoy your trip ahead!

Made in the USA
Monee, IL
25 February 2025